BEGINNING THE GOOD NEWS

Francis J. Moloney, S.D.B.

BEGINNING
THE GOOD NEWS

A Narrative Approach

A Liturgical Press Book

THE LITURGICAL PRESS
Collegeville, Minnesota

Beginning the Good News: A Narrative Approach

First published in 1992
by St. Paul Publications
Homebush, Australia
© Francis J. Moloney, S.D.B., 1992

Cover painting: Jesus by Agar Loche, PDDM, 1979, © 1988 JESUS Epipress, Milan, Italy
Front cover design: Bruno Colombari S.S.P.

Typeset and printed by Society of St. Paul, Wantirna South, Victoria.

St. Paul Publications is an activity of the Priests and Brothers of the Society of St. Paul who proclaim the Gospel through the media of social communication.

Published in the United States of America and in Canada by The Liturgical Press, Collegeville, Minnesota 56321. Printed in the United States of America.

1	2	3	4	5	6	7	8

Library of Congress Cataloging-in-Publication Data

Moloney, Francis J.
    Beginning the good news : a narrative approach / Francis J. Moloney.
        p.   cm.
    Originally published: Homebush, Australia : St. Paul Publications, 1992.
    Includes bibliographical references (p.).
    ISBN 0-8146-2265-8
    1. Bible. N.T. Gospels—Criticism, Narrative. I. Title.
BS2555.2.M585   1995
226'.066—dc20   94-45066
                                                                CIP

For Deborah
with thanks

Although now long estranged
Man is not wholly lost nor wholly changed.
Dis-graced he may be, yet is not de-throned,
and keeps the rags of lordship once he owned:
Man, the Sub-creator, the refracted Light
through whom is splintered from a single White
to many hues, and endlessly combined
in living shapes that move from mind to mind.

J.R.R. Tolkien

CONTENTS

ABBREVIATIONS

AB	Anchor Bible.
AnBib	Analecta Biblica.
BAGD	W. Bauer – W.F. Arndt – F.W. Gingrich – F.W. Danker, *A Greek-English Lexicon of the New Testament and Other Early Christian Literature* (Chicago: University Press, 1979²).
BJ	Bible de Jérusalem.
BibScRel	Biblioteca di Scienze Religiose.
BTB	*Biblical Theology Bulletin.*
BZ	*Biblische Zeitschrift.*
CBQ	*The Catholic Biblical Quarterly.*
DRev	*The Downside Review.*
EB	Etudes Bibliques.
FRLANT	Forshungen zur Religion und Literatur des Alten und Neuen Testaments.
GBSNT	Guides to Biblical Scholarship. New Testament Series.
GNS	Good News Studies.
HTCNT	Herder's Theological Commentary on the New Testament.

HTKNT	Herders theologische Kommentar zum Neuen Testament.
ICC	International Critical Commentary.
Int	*Interpretation.*
IRT	Issues in Religion and Theology.
JB	The Jerusalem Bible.
JBCE	The Joint Board of Christian Education of Australia and New Zealand.
JBL	*Journal of Biblical Literature.*
JSNTSS	Journal for the Study of the New Testament Supplement Series.
JSOTSS	Journal for the Study of the Old Testament Supplement Series.
Jud	*Judaica.*
LAS	Libreria Ateneo Salesiano.
LumVie	*Lumière et Vie.*
LSJ	H. Lidell – R. Scott – H.S. Jones, *A Greek-English Lexicon* (Oxford: Clarendon, 1968).
LXX	The Septuagint.
MT	The Masoretic Text.
NCB	New Century Bible.
NICNT	New International Commentary on the New Testament.
NIGTC	The New International Greek Testament Commentary.
NJB	The New Jerusalem Bible.
NJBC	R.E. Brown – J.A. Fitzmyer – R.E. Murphy (eds.), *The New Jerome Biblical Commentary* (Englewood Cliffs: Prentice Hall, 1990).
NovT	*Novum Testamentum.*
NovTSupp	Supplements to Novum Testamentum.
NRSV	B.M. Metzger – R.E. Murphy (eds.), *The New Oxford Annotated Bible with the Apocryphal/Deuterocanonical Books. New Revised Standard Version* (New York: Oxford University Press, 1991).
NTAbh	Neutestamentliche Abhandlungen.

NRT	*Nouvelle Revue Théologique.*
NTM	New Testament Message.
NTS	*New Testament Studies.*
OBS	Oxford Bible Series.
öTB	Ökumenischer Taschenbuchkommentar zum Neuen Testament.
Pac	*Pacifica.*
RevQ	*Revue de Qumran.*
RSV	Revised Standard Version.
SBLMS	Society for Biblical Literature Monograph Series.
SBT	Studies in Biblical Theology.
SCM	Students' Christian Movement.
ScEs	*Science et Esprit.*
Sem	*Semeia.*
SJT	*Scottish Journal of Theology.*
SNTSMS	Society for New Testament Studies Monograph Series.
SPCK	Society for the Promotion of Christian Knowledge.
THZNT	Theologische Handkommentar zum Neuen Testament.
TOB	Traduction Oecuménique de la Bible.
TPINTC	Trinity Press International New Testament Commentaries.
TS	*Theological Studies.*
TDNT	G. Kittel – G. Friedrich (eds.), *Theological Dictionary of the New Testament* (10 vols.; Grand Rapids: Eerdmans, 1964-76).
UBSGNT	*The Greek New Testament* (London/New York: United Bible Societies, 1983[3]).
WBC	Word Biblical Commentary.
ZBG	M. Zerwick, *Biblical Greek Illustrated by Examples* (Rome: Biblical Institute Press, 1963).

PREFACE

The Melbourne College of Divinity Lectures offer an Australian scholar the opportunity to address issues which reflect, however broadly, contemporary theological scholarship. Although the Melbourne College of Divinity has been an important seat of theological education in Australia and the Pacific since the turn of the century, these occasional lectures are a recent initiative. Begun as an experiment in 1985, they have now become a presence of the Melbourne College of Divinity in the public domain.

The scholars who preceded me as the invited lecturers have set the tone – and the standard. Prof. Gerald O'Collins, of the Gregorian University, was the first M.C.D. lecturer in 1985. He raised the question of doing Christology within an Australian context.[1] Prof. Ian Breward

---

1   G. O'Collins, *Jesus Today. Doing Christology in an Australian Context* (Melbourne: Collins Dove, 1985).

of the Uniting Faculty of Theology delivered a stimulat-
ing series of lectures on Australia's religious history in
1988. In this way the Melbourne College of Divinity
marked the celebration of the bi-centenary of European
presence in Australia.[2]

I was privileged to be invited to give the 1991 lectures,
and happy that the discipline of Biblical Studies was seen
as sufficiently relevant in contemporary Australia to make
an offering to this important series. I had no difficulty
in deciding that I would deliver lectures based upon the
recent interest in narrative criticism. Story plays a role
in many contemporary academic disciplines; some of them
seemingly far removed from matters theological.[3] It took
me longer to decide which Gospel texts I should 'read'.
There is always a temptation to go to the 'good stories',
well known by people who have little knowledge of matters biblical, in an attempt to maintain interest in a public lecture series. Some excellent 'stories' came to mind:
Mark's version of the Gerasene demoniac (Mk 5:1-21),
Matthew's parable of the unmerciful servant (Mt
18:23-35), the meeting of Jesus and Zacchaeus in Luke

2   I. Breward, *Australia: 'The Most Godless Place under the Sun?'* (Melbourne:
    Beacon Hill Books, 1988).
3   For a survey of the growth of interest in narrative, see T.W. Tilley, *Story
    Theology* (Theology and Life 12; Michael Glazier: Wilmington, 1985)
    pp. 18-54. By 'narrative criticism' I intend a synchronic reading of the text,
    aided by both the traditional historical-critical approach and the newer
    methods imported from literary criticism. There is a temptation to opt for
    either 'history' or 'literature' which must be resisted. For my method, see
    F.J. Moloney, 'Narrative Criticism of the Gospels', *Pac* 4 (1991) 180-201.
    As my main concern is a reading of the text, my approach is neither 'post-
    modern' nor purely reader-oriented. On this, quite different, approach see
    G.A. Phillips (ed.), *Poststructural Criticism and the Bible: Text/History/
    Discourse* (Semeia 51; Atlanta: Scholars Press, 1990), especially the articles
    by G.A. Phillips, 'Exegesis as Critical Praxis: Reclaiming History and Text
    from a Postmodern Perspective' (pp. 7-49) and F.W. Burnett, 'Postmodern

(Lk 19:1-10) or the curing of the man born blind in the Fourth Gospel (Jn 9:1-41). But I was looking for some common ground linking a narrative chosen from each Gospel. Narrative criticism devotes considerable attention to the temporal flow of a narrative.[4] Out of respect for this important element in the proper understanding of a narrative, I decided to read the 'beginnings' of each Gospel. In that way I did not have to presuppose too much of my audience's knowledge of the flow of the narrative of each particular Gospel up to that point. Also, 'beginnings' have interested literary critics for some time.[5] Having made that decision, and having already begun the lecture series, I was encouraged to find that the current number of *Semeia*, an experimental journal for biblical criticism, was devoted to the same question.[6]

The first lecture is dedicated to a brief historical overview of the changing fashions and the changing hermeneutical perspectives in critical New Testament scholarship which led to the current interest in narrative criticism. Each of the following lectures 'reads' the beginnings of the Four Gospels, all of which can justifiably be called prologues. I have attempted a reading of Mark 1:1-13; Matthew 1-2; Luke 1-2 and John 1:1-18. I close with an epilogue which did not form part of the lecture series.

Biblical Exegesis: The Eve of Historical Criticism' (pp. 51-80). On the whole question, see S.D. Moore, *Literary Criticism and the Gospels. The Theoretical Challange* (New Haven: Yale University Press, 1989).

4   On this, see the magisterial work of G. Genette, *Narrative Discourse. An Essay in Method* (Ithaca: Cornell University Press, 1980) pp. 33-85.

5   See M.C. Parsons, 'Reading a Beginning/Beginning a Reading. Tracing Literary Theory on Narrative Openings', *Sem* 52 (1990) 11-31 and Idem, 'How Narratives Begin: A Bibliography', *Sem* 52 (1990) 34-41.

6   D.E. Smith (ed.), *How Gospels Began* (Semeia 52; Atlanta: Scholars Press, 1990). I have been able to incorporate these studies into my research, even though they were not available to me at the time of the lecture series.

I have reproduced the studies in a form close to the original lecture, although I have added documentation for the publication of the papers, so that an interested reader may further pursue some of the issues raised. As well as the contribution which I hope the published version of the lectures may make to the interpretation of the Gospels, I also hope that it may serve as an introduction to the contemporary interest in a narrative approach to Gospel criticism.

A recent reflection on the reception of the Bible in contemporary society asked four questions: 'Is there an audience for the Bible today? If there is an audience, does it have some basic attitude to life in place when it opens the Bible? What does this audience think and believe about the Bible? What might encourage this audience to more frequent, deeper, and more enriching encounters with the Bible?'[7] The large attendances and the interest aroused by the 1991 Melbourne College of Divinity Lectures indicate that all four questions still need to be asked. The studies of 'beginnings' which follow are an attempt to contribute to a deeper, more enriching encounter with the Bible.

I would like to express my gratitude to the Melbourne College of Divinity, which honoured me with the invitation to deliver these lectures. I would like to thank Nerina M. Zanardo, F.S.P., who read the following studies in their various redactions, first as lectures and then as studies for publication. They are dedicated to another long-standing and loyal friend, Deborah Browne, who adds a great deal of joy, encouragement and affection to my

---

7   E.A. Wcela, 'Who Do You Say That They Are? Reflections on the Biblical Audience Today', *CBQ* 53 (1991) 1-17. I cite from p. 2.

life. The verse from J.R.R. Tolkien is taken from a letter he wrote in the late 1930's (and thus the use of 'Man') to a person who described myth and fairy tales as 'lies'.[8]

Catholic Theological College   *Francis J. Moloney, SDB*
Clayton
Victoria 3168 Australia
28th May 1991

---

8   It is found in J.R.R. Tolkien, *Tree and Leaf* (London: Unwin Books, 1964) p. 49. This slim volume contains Tolkein's remarkable essay 'On Fairy Stories' (pp. 9-70) and one of his early short stories, 'Leaf by Niggle' (pp. 71-92). I am grateful to A.J. Kelly, C.Ss.R, for making it available to me.

1 | A STORY WHICH LED TO STORY

Late in the eighteenth century, fragments from a private reflection written by a little-known teacher of oriental languages from Hamburg, Hermann Samuel Reimarus (1694-1768), were published by Gotthold Lessing (1729-1781) under the title, *Fragments by an Unknown Person* (1774-78).[1] Reimarus had honestly sought, in his 'private fragments', to quiet his conscience in the light of the English Deists' attacks upon the traditional use of the Gospels. The Deists pointed out the many difficulties and contradictions found in the Bible and Reimarus looked again at early Christian history. Reimarus' reconstruction of that history led him to conclude that the task was 'completely to separate what the apostles present in their writings from what Jesus himself actually said and taught during his lifetime'.[2]

---

1   Available in English in C.H. Talbert (ed.), *Reimarus: Fragments* (Philadelphia: Fortress, 1970).
2   As cited by W.G. Kümmel, *The New Testament. The History of the Investigation of Its Problems* (London: SCM, 1973) p. 89.

However unwittingly, Reimarus opened a flood gate, through which the waters are still flowing.[3] Directly related to Reimarus' *Fragments* and particularly influential was the ground-breaking work of David Strauss (1808-1874), who introduced the concept of 'myth' into a study of the life of Jesus, and Ferdinand Christian Baur (1792-1860) who, in many publications, attempted to situate the various New Testament writings within the social and religious conflicts of the first and second century. These are the foundation stones upon which contemporary Gospel criticism has been constructed.

The critical work of these scholars raised the question of the relationship between the life of the historical Jesus and the way it is reported in the Gospels. The introduction of the concept of 'myth' and situating the New Testament writings within the historical, social and religious contexts which produced them began a landslide. The Gospels were the products of a given community at a given time; Paul can only be understood as part of a dialectic that was the early Jewish-Christian Church. The stories of the Gospels were never meant to be pen-pictures of what Jesus did on this or that occasion during his life. Both his teaching and the subsequent teaching of Paul on moral and disciplinary matters reflect the problems of a late first

---

3   For surveys, see W.G. Kümmel, *The New Testament*; R.F. Collins, *Introduction to the New Testament* (Garden City: Doubleday, 1983); R.M. Grant – D. Tracy, *A Short History of the Interpretation of the Bible* (Philadelphia: Fortress, 1984²) pp. 100-133; R. Morgan – J. Barton, *Biblical Interpretation* (OBS; Oxford: University Press, 1988) pp. 44-132; S. Neill – N.T. Wright, *The Interpretation of the New Testament, 1861-1986* (New York: Oxford University Press, 1988²). Important more specialised studies are: H. Harris, *The Tübingen School* (Oxford: Clarendon Press, 1975); H. Frei, *The Eclipse of Biblical Narrative. A Study in Eighteenth and Nineteenth Century Hermeneutics* (New Haven: Yale, 1974).

century Church coping with its break from the traditional *mores* of the Law, or facing new situations in the Graeco-Roman world of which Jesus had never dreamt. When the History of Religions School joined the fray at the turn of the century it was even suggested that the concept of the saving death and resurrection of Jesus Christ had come into Christianity from the Mystery Religions, and that much of Paul and the Fourth Gospel came from early Gnosticism.

Parallel with the questions raised by the rationalist critique, the historical-critical study of the Bible was greatly assisted by some spectacular discoveries. Keys were found which unlocked previously closed and mysterious languages and cultures (for example, the Rosetta Stone [1799], Tell el-Amarna [1887], the Cairo Genizah [1890-1898], Nag Hammadi [1945], Rash Shamra [1946], Qumran [1948]).[4] Such discoveries led to a serious comparative study of earlier forms of Judaism and other ancient religions. This study shed even greater light on the world which had produced the Bible, and libraries of *scholarly* work which debate these questions are now to be found in the great Universities of Europe and the United States. But what of the faith and practice of the Churches? Have the Christian Churches ever recovered from the shock of Reimarus, Strauss and Baur?

FORM CRITICISM

The development of the various 'methods' of critical New Testament scholarship since the liberals of the 19th century,

---

4   See the survey of J. Finegan, *Light from the Ancient Past. The Archeological Background to the Hebrew-Christian Religion* (2 vols.; Princeton: Princeton University Press, 1959[2]).

into the History of Religions School and the still unresolved debates over the place of eschatology in the earliest Church eventually produced the discipline called form criticism.[5] Excellent philologists, products of a solid training in the newer methods, working within the context of the rich theological discussions aroused by the young Karl Barth (1886-1968) and his contemporaries,[6] Karl Ludwig Schmidt (1891-1956), Martin Dibelius (1883-1947) and Rudolf Bultmann (1884-1976) all wrote books between 1919 and 1921 which set the agenda for subsequent study of the Gospels.[7] Detailed analysis of the Gospels showed that they were the result of a practice of gathering brief Jesus-stories in a given community, modifying them when needed and, in those instances where no suitable story was available in the tradition, creating them. The stories were accepted, modified or created to address the needs of the Christian community in question. Dibelius and especially Bultmann indicated the close parallels which exist between the various literary forms of Gospel passages (apothegms, dominical sayings, miracle stories, historical stories and legends, to use Bultmann's classification) and the parallel forms found in contemporary

5   An important forerunner of both Form and Redaction Criticism was W. Wrede. Already in 1901 his work, *Das Messiasgeheimnis in den Evangelien* raised the question of both the situation in the life of the community (Form Criticism) which called for the theological activity of the Evangelist Mark to create the literary fiction of the messianic secret (Redaction Criticism). This work is available in English: W. Wrede, *The Messianic Secret* (Cambridge & London: James Clarke, 1971).

6   On this, see W. Kümmel, *The New Testament*, pp. 363-404.

7   K.L. Schmidt, *Der Rahmen der Geschichte Jesu. Literarkritische Untersuchungen zur Ältesten Jesusüberlieferung* (Darmstadt: Wissenschaftliche Buchgesellschaft, 1964) Original: 1919; M. Dibelius, *From Tradition to Gospel* (Cambridge & London: James Clarke, 1971) Original: 1919; R. Bultmann, *The History of the Synoptic Tradition* (Oxford: Blackwell, 1968) Original: 1921. See W.G. Kümmel, *The New Testament*, pp. 325-341.

religious and secular literature. From there they moved easily (most would nowadays say, too easily) to identify the situation in the life of the community (the origin of the much-used expression *Sitz im Leben*) which caused the community to accept, modify or create these passages.

Still reeling from the radical scholarship of the previous century and the chaos created by the First World War, the established Churches reacted to form criticism with shock and anger. The form critics situated the origins of each single pericope in the Gospel within the life of an early Christian community resolving its own theological, missionary and inner-community problems (to mention only a few) towards the end of the first century. There was a fear that historical-critical biblical scholarship had taken the Gospels as Jesus' life-story away from the already traumatised preacher. Where were they to go now for their Christian doctrines and ethics, if they could not point to some episode from the life of Jesus Christ as its source? Yet the form critics, for all their prejudices and errors of judgment,[8] showed that each Gospel was a book of the Church. Indeed, they showed that it was a book of 'the Churches'. Although the contemporary preacher is not the reader to whom the Gospel was originally directed, he or she stands in a Christian tradition which is addressed by a story of Jesus written in and for a Christian Church.

Looking back, it appears to me that it was not so much the form critics who caused difficulties for the ongoing

8 For example, Bultmann's whole project is deeply influenced by his radical commitment to the Lutheran agenda of *sola fide*. See the critical studies of A. Malet, *The Thought of Rudolf Bultmann* (New York: Doubleday, 1971); J. Painter, *Theology as Hermeneutics. Rudolf Bultmann's Interpretation of the History of Jesus* (Sheffield: The Almond Press, 1987). See also the comprehensive study (not without its own prejudices) of E. Guttgemanns, *Candid Questions Concerning Gospel Form Criticism* (The Pickwick Press, 1975).

presence of the living voice of the Gospel in the Church, but the churchmen and the preachers. Despite the speculative nature of many results of the form critical approach to the Gospels up to the Second World War, it had shown that these documents were produced by believing people for belief. The Gospels are not primarily historical records, but confessions of belief. Somehow the value of this discovery was only rarely seen. It was more comfortable for the preachers to tell the old stories as if they happened exactly as they were reported than to use the Word to summon people to a deeper commitment to a Christian life addressed by the narratives in the Gospels. But which method is truer to the Word itself? Is it all that offensive to claim that Gospel narratives are not only narratives, but also kerygma: proclamation?[9]

REDACTION CRITICISM

The form critical analysis of the Gospels eventually led to an important breakthrough, initiated formally by Hans Conzelmann's study of Luke in the post-war period (1953). If the situation in the life of a given community had led to the formation of each pericope in the tradition, what led to the eventual construction of each Gospel narrative as a whole? As Conzelmann himself put it: 'We must make it plain ... that our aim is to elucidate Luke's work in its present form, not to enquire about possible sources or into the historical facts which provide the material. A variety of sources does not necessarily imply a similar variety in the thought and composition of the author. How

---

9   I am well aware that many radical form critics claimed that it was not 'also kerygma' but *only* kerygma.

did it come about, that he brought together these particular materials? Was he able to imprint on them his
own views?'[10] It was not only that the various parts of
the Gospel reflected some original faith-response of the
early Church to its world, but the whole document did
so. We were now able to see that not only was Paul the
author of a coherent theological system. So were Mark,
Matthew, Luke and John.

While this method, which devoted its attention to the
Gospel as a whole, caused an initial sigh of relief from
the preachers, they soon found that the redaction critics
had not dispensed with form criticism. The redaction
critics had learnt from their elders that the Gospels were
collections of different pearls from the early Church.[11]
They went one step further to trace the four different
strings that gathered those pearls, recognised as such by
the form critics, into necklaces of different shapes. Indeed, within the Synoptic Gospels, many of the pearls
taken separately and compared synoptically are identical,
but the final shape of each Gospel's use of those pearls is
different. It was the way in which the pearls were assem-
bled which produced our four-fold Gospel tradition.[12]

Redaction Criticism was helpful to the preacher, insisting much less on the historical origins of the various

10 H. Conzelmann, *The Theology of St. Luke* (London: Faber & Faber, 1960)
    p. 9.
11 This much-used analogy was first coined by K.L. Schmidt, *Die Rahmen
    der Geschichte Jesu*.
12 Indeed, it produced many gospels, but only four eventually entered the
    'canon' of the Christian Church. For the 'other gospels', see E. Hennecke
    − W. Schneemelcher (ed.), *The New Testament Apocrypha* (London: SCM,
    1963) Vol. 1. See also H. Koester, *Ancient Christian Gospels. Their History
    and Development* (London: SCM, 1990).

pericope which formed the Gospel and more on the theological message of the document as a whole. Yet the Christian Churches have found it difficult to assimilate the rich results of four decades of redaction critical study because it still traces an early Christian theologian behind the Gospel story, as well as Jesus of Nazareth.

It must be said that the erudition of the past 150 years of historical-critical biblical scholarship has not made a great impact upon Christian preaching and practice. Most Christian Churches have settled for the tradition rather than the disturbing relevance of the Word itself. They inherited an age-old method of interpreting the Scriptures passed down from the great commentaries of Origen, Chrysostom, Augustine and the other Fathers, both from antiquity, and from the reform, especially Luther and Calvin.[13]

The radical break from a traditional way of reading the Gospels which follows from an acceptance of the methods devised by the form critics and the redaction critics raises a crucial question to the Churches who use the Gospels as Sacred Scripture: is the Bible an infallible word thundering down from the heavens, or the Word of God in the words of men and women? This question is posed in terms of the *origins* of the Word of God as we have it in the Bible. Both form and redaction criticism raise the issue: where does it come from?

The problems raised by the Enlightenment and the English Deists who ridiculed the claim that the Bible could possibly be the Word *of God* were eventually

---

13 The methods of patristic, medieval and reformation interpretation (which have their own problems) are outlined in R.M. Grant − D. Tracy, *A Short History*, pp. 39-99.

answered through a closer study of the world which *stood behind the text*. The historical question has justifiably dominated biblical criticism from the 19th century down to our own time. There are also serious theological questions raised by the historical-critical approach to the Bible. It is one thing to claim that the Bible is the Word of God in the limited and necessarily fallible words of men and women, but how does one then defend the central place of the Bible in the Christian Churches? If its awkwardness and apparent contradictions are to be explained in terms of its fragile and historically conditioned human origins, how can it still remain, in some way, the Word *of God*?

This is another question arising from modern biblical scholarship, and reflection upon it, which is too often simply ignored. Many significant theologians and most ecclesiastical bodies responsible for authentic doctrine, even those from traditions which claim to be living exclusively 'under the word', simply opt for what has always been said and done, no matter how seriously it is questioned by a critical study of the Bible.[14] As Raymond Brown has described the situation: 'If the biblical scholar is going to insist on the freedom to play with his new-fangled toys of language and literary form, he is to be kept in a playpen and not let out to disturb the good order of the theological household'.[15]

The gap which has developed between the scholar at his desk and the Christian in the street has led, over the

---

14 On this, see F.J. Moloney, *A Body Broken for a Broken People. Eucharist in the New Testament* (Melbourne: Collins Dove, 1990), pp. 5-18.

15 R.E. Brown, *The Virginal Conception and the Bodily Resurrection of Jesus* (London: Geoffrey Chapman, 1973) p. 6. I have changed the tenses into the present.

last decade, to a more systematic questioning of the
relevance of the historical-critical method. Does it have
anything to say to the theological household or to the
Church at large? One often hears it said that it is 'bank-
rupt' or that it has outlived its usefulness.[16] In the light
of this sometimes strident criticism, one might ask if traditional historical-critical Gospel scholarship has any further role to play in the Christian Church.[17]

Biblical scholars have rightly used the historical-critical
method as a tool to ensure that the world *behind the text*
is not forgotten in the appropriation of the world *in the
text*. Form criticism and redaction criticism have been
developed to force the Church to preach the Word of God
more honestly, to proclaim what it originally proclaimed,
not to make it merely serve the Church's own purposes.[18]
But if some have made a rigid application of historical-
critical methods the last word, the *non plus ultra*, then
they have been wrong to do so.[19]

16 See, for example, A.L. Nations, 'Historical Criticism and the Current
    Methodological Crisis', *SJT* 36 (1983) 59-71; E. Schüssler-Fiorenza, 'The
    Ethics of Interpretation: De-Centering Biblical Scholarship', *JBL* 107 (1988)
    3-17; A. Stock, 'The Limits of Historical-Critical Exegesis', *BTB* 13 (1983)
    28-31; W. Wink, *Transforming Bible Study* (London: SCM, 1981). The whole
    number of *Communio* 13 (1986) was dedicated to a generally negative
    assessment of contemporary Catholic use of the historical-critical method.
17 For a *systematic* refusal to use scholarly methods and the results of two
    centuries of research, see the various volumes (beautifully produced in the
    English version by Four Courts, Dublin) of *The Navarre Bible*. One finds
    a surface reading of the text commented upon by a selective reading of
    the Fathers of the Church, the scholastic tradition, the Popes and J. Escrivá.
    Modern critical scholarship is completely ignored.
18 The practice of all the Churches to read the world *in the text* in a way
    which has little or nothing to do with that world is too well known to
    need documentation. See, however, E.V. McKnight, *Post-Modern Use of the
    Bible. The Emergence of Reader-Oriented Criticism* (Nashville: Abingdon,
    1988) pp. 29-49.
19 See J.A. Fitzmyer, 'Historical Criticism: Its Role in Biblical Interpretation
    and Church Life', *TS* (1989) 244-259, esp. pp. 252-255.

LITERARY CRITICISM

Biblical scholarship has gradually come to appreciate more fully that there are more than two 'worlds' involved in the interpretation of an ancient text. Historical-critical scholarship has devoted almost 200 years to the rediscovery of the *world behind the text,* so that there be no abuse of the *world in the text.* Now more attention needs to be devoted to the world *in front of the text.* Scholars are currently responding to this need by developing new methods which concentrate upon the reader of the text.[20]

After a brief flurry of structuralism from France, which did not make a great deal of direct impact upon German or English-speaking scholars,[21] recent New Testament scholarship has become more concerned with literary criticism of the Bible in the strict sense of its being literature. Many of the principles of structuralist literary criticism are present in the contemporary approach,[22] but there is now a greater interest in approaching each single document, however limited and flawed it might be, as a work of art.

---

20 See E.V. McKnight, *The Reader and the Bible. An Introduction to Literary Criticism* (Philadelphia: Fortress, 1985); Idem, *Post-Modern*; R. Morgan – J. Barton, *Biblical Interpretation,* pp. 133-296. See also M. Coleridge, 'The Necessary Angel: Imagination and the Bible', *Pac* 1 (1988) 171-188.

21 Structuralism had its origins in anthropology, and especially in the work of Claude Levy-Strauss. Its chief and best advocate in the English-speaking world is Donald Patte. See, for example, D. Patte, D. and A. Patte, *Structural Exegesis: From Theory to Practice* (Philadelphia: Fortress Press, 1978); D. Patte, *Paul's Faith and the Power of the Gospel. A Structural Introduction to the Pauline Letters* (Philadelphia: Fortress Press, 1983); Idem, *The Gospel According to Matthew. A Structural Commentary on Matthew's Faith* (Philadelphia: Fortress Press, 1987). See the recent assessment of structuralism from a postmodern perspective in G.A. Phillips, 'Exegesis as Critical Praxis', *Sem* 51 (1990) 15-19.

22 Especially evident in the influential work of S. Chatman, *Story and Discourse. Narrative Structure in Fiction and Film* (Ithaca: Cornell University Press, 1978).

This has led to a narrative critical study of the Gospels. Such an approach has been pursued in literary circles for some time. Contemporary Gospel studies are showing an increasing interest in what has come to be known as narrative criticism. Adapting and applying theories of narrative developed by literary theorists, Old Testament scholars were the first to seize upon this possible approach, given the large amount of narrative text found within the pages of the Bible.[23] New Testament critics have not been slow to follow.[24]

Behind each 'story' there is a *real author* who has a definite group of people in mind as he or she tells the story. Thus, there is an intended *real reader*. Neither of these figures is *in* the story itself. One produces it and the other takes it in hand to read it, or listens to it. An author constructs a narrative as a means to communicate a message to an audience, but if, by some strange quirk of history, the narrative itself was totally destroyed and forgotten, the real author and the real reader would still exist or have existed as historical persons.

Narratives have many features. They have deliberately contrived plots and characters who interact throughout the story along a certain time line, through a sequence

---

23 Perhaps the most widely read and influential contribution has been that of M. Sternberg, *The Poetics of Biblical Narrative. Ideological Literature and the Drama of Reading* (Indiana Literary Biblical Series; Bloomington: Indiana University Press, 1985). See also R. Alter, *The Art of Biblical Narrative* (New York: Basic Books, 1981); G. Josipovici, *The Book of God. A Response to the Bible* (New Haven: Yale University Press, 1988). A good synthesis can be found in S. Bar-Efrat, *Narrative Art in the Bible* (JSOTSS; Sheffield: Almond Press, 1989).
24 For a comprehensive study and an original contribution to the discussion, see S.D. Moore, *Literary Criticism and the Gospels.* See also M.A. Powell, *What Is Narrative Criticism?* (GBSNT; Minneapolis: Fortress Press, 1990).

of events. An author devises certain rhetorical features to hold plot and character together so that the reader will not miss the author's point of view.[25] These rhetorical features are *in* the narrative. Although narrative theoreticians dispute the exactness of the scheme, one can broadly claim that the communication between a real author and a real reader who are *outside* the text takes place through an implied author, a narrator, a narratee and an implied reader who are *inside* the text.[26] The following diagram indicates how these constitutive elements of a narrative relate to one another.[27]

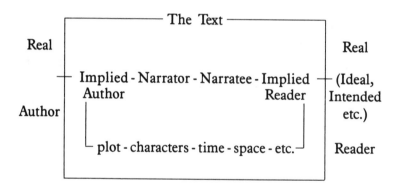

This is hardly the place for a full scale introduction to the theory of narrative criticism and its application

25 S.D. Moore, *Literary Criticism*, p. 14: 'Narrative criticism is a story-preoccupied gospel criticism. Being preoccupied with story means, most of all, being preoccupied with *plot* and *character*'.
26 For a schematic presentation of this communication theory, see S. Chatman, *Story and Discourse*, p. 266.
27 This diagram, which I have modified, is taken from S. Chatman, *Story and Discourse*, p. 151. For more complete diagrams, see *ibid.*, p. 267 and R.A. Culpepper, *The Anatomy of the Fourth Gospel. A Study in Literary Design* (Foundation and Facets; Philadelphia: Fortress, 1983) p. 6.

to the narratives of the New Testament.[28] The four Gospel readings of 'beginnings' which follow will focus, largely, upon the literary features found in the narrative. I will pay no attention to Mark, Matthew, Luke and John whoever they may have been. I will attempt to trace, via the literary features of the story-telling, the communication which is taking place *in the narrative* between an author and a reader. As such, some further clarification of what narrative critics mean when they write and speak of an author and a reader is called for.[29]

After four decades of intense scholarship, redaction critics now speak with considerable confidence of the theological perspective, or point of view, of Matthew, Mark, Luke and John, whoever they may have been in real life. But how do the critics know? The authors of the Gospels are long since dead. One can only *guess* what the theological point of view of the real authors of our Gospel texts may have been. The authors and their opinions are, in themselves, *outside our scientific control.*

28 For some initial Gospel studies along these lines, see D. Rhoads – D. Michie, *Mark as Story. An Introduction to the Narrative of a Gospel* (Philadelphia: Fortress, 1982); B. van Iersel, *Reading Mark* (Edinburgh: T. & T. Clark, 1989); J.D. Kingsbury, *Matthew as Story* (Philadelphia: Fortress, 1988[2]); R.C. Tannehill, *The Narrative Unity of Luke-Acts* (2 vols.; Foundation and Facets; Philadelphia/Minneapolis, Fortress, 1986-90); J.N. Aletti, *L'art de raconter Jésus Christ* (Paris: Seuil, 1989); R.A. Culpepper, *The Anatomy of the Fourth Gospel*. The theoretical works which have influenced me most are G. Genette, *Narrative Discourse; Idem, Narrative Discourse Revisited* (Ithaca: Cornell University Press, 1988); S. Chatman, *Story and Discourse,* W. Iser, *The Act of Reading. A Theory of Aesthetic Response* (London: Routledge & Kegan Paul, 1978); S. Rimmon-Kenan, *Narrative Fiction: Contemporary Poetics* (New Accents: London: Methuen, 1983), and W.C. Booth, *The Rhetoric of Fiction* (Chicago: University of Chicago Press, 1983[2]). See now F.J. Moloney, 'Narrative Criticism of the Gospels', *Pac* 4 (1991) 181-201.
29 Narrative criticism, of course, is much more far-reaching. See the bibliography given in the previous footnote for some further indications. See also M.A. Powell, *What Is Narrative Criticism?*

The only objective reality to which the critic can look is *the text itself*.

It is from the text that one can come to some idea of the point of view of an author − but which author? It is perfectly possible for an author to write a narrative which communicates a point of view that is not a reflection of his own situation in life, his humour, personality, or personal experience. As George Steiner has recently said in his remarkable essay, *Real Presences*: 'Aristophanes may, at heart, have been the saddest of men − the which proposal is itself a piece of romanticised inversion. Our persuasion that some deep turbulence of spirit and sexuality attended the composition of *King Lear and Timon of Athens* may be nothing but trivial rationalisation. We have no shred of evidence either way'.[30] What the first-century author of a story of the life, teaching, death and resurrection of Jesus might have thought about any issue can never finally be rediscovered. We can only trace the point of view of the text itself.

There is, therefore, an author *in the text*. Whatever the perspective of a historical flesh-and-blood author may have been, we can only claim to trace the theological point of view of an author in the text itself. Such an author is generally called *the implied author*.[31] This feature of narrative is not a historical person, however well it may or may not reflect the choices of that figure from the past who may be called *the real author*. Unlike some

---

30 G. Steiner, *Real Presences. Is there anything in what we say?* (London: Faber & Faber, 1989) p. 169.

31 W. Booth, *Rhetoric*, pp. 73-74, defines the implied author: 'the intuitive apprehension of a completed artistic whole; the chief value to which *this* implied author is committed, regardless of what party his creator belongs to in real life, is that which is expressed by the total form'.

contemporary narratives, it can generally be assumed (but never proved) that the real author *of* and the implied author *in* New Testament narratives speak with the same voice.

Similarly, one can ask the redaction critic how sure he or she can be about the original *intended readership* of any particular narrative. Flesh-and-blood historical real readers are outside the control of real authors. How I might respond to a narrative in any of the Gospels may vary from day to day, depending on any number of circumstances. We are well aware of the numerous circumstances which affect, for better or worse, the reading process. Yet, *within the narrative* there is a reader addressed by the implied author. As the narrative unfolds, the reader is gradually provided with information and experiences which such a reader cannot avoid.[32] This reader is shaped by the desires of the author and emerges as the text unfolds. Thus, one can speak of a literary construct within the narrative itself, whose responses are totally controlled by the implied author. Such a 'reader' is generally called *the implied reader*. The implied reader is not a historical person. Historically there are only real readers. The implied reader is a heuristic device produced by the unfolding narrative. By tracing the developing knowledge and experience of the implied reader as the text unfolds, I am better able to appreciate the temporal flow of the narrative. Stanley Fish has described the use of the implied reader by a narrative critic as follows:

> The basis of the method is a consideration of the *temporal* flow of the reading experience, and it is assumed

---

32 Narrative critics talk about the affective and cognitive effects of the narrative on the implied reader.

that the reader responds in terms of that flow and not to the whole utterance. That is, in an utterance of any length, there is a point at which the reader has taken in only the first word, and then the second, and then the third, and so on, and the report of what happens to the reader is always a report of what happened *to that point*.[33]

As the readings of the 'beginnings' of the four Gospel stories which follow is an attempt to trace the implied reader emerging from those narratives, a further point not made by Fish needs to be made. The implied reader is a literary construct, a virginal reader who gradually emerges from the unfolding narrative, shaped by the implied author, knowing only what has been read so far. But the implied reader can also move backwards to recall events already narrated. Although totally ignorant of what is yet to come, the implied reader has been formed and informed by what has been read so far.[34]

But is it possible that the implied reader in the Christian Gospels has no knowledge or experience of the story of Jesus of Nazareth and Christian life and practices? The direct importation of literary scholarship into New Testament studies has sometimes presupposed such an implied reader. Yet the implied author takes it for granted that

---

33 S. Fish, *Is There a Text in This Class? The Authority of Interpretative Communities* (Cambridge: Harvard University Press, 1980) pp. 26-27.
34 As we are dealing with a literary construct, it is without gender. However, as the implied reader is credited with both affective and cognitive experiences, a more personal pronoun is sometimes demanded. This is difficult. Given the present state of the English language, I may often repeat the noun 'reader' more than is necessary or sometimes revert to the passive, to avoid a male or female pronoun. I will occasionally write 'he or she'. I am aware that this overloads the text somewhat, but I am unwilling to use the increasingly popular (especially in the USA) 's/he'.

the reader knows many things already. The implied reader knows Greek! The implied reader is able (especially in the Fourth Gospel) to understand double meanings behind Greek words, subtle ironies, etc. Much is presupposed of the implied reader. The unexplained use of certain Jewish messianic categories, religious customs and the geography of Palestine indicates that all this (and much more) is taken as known. In short, one must grant that the implied reader knows everything that the implied author does not explain. The implied reader in each Gospel story may be credited with some knowledge of the Jesus story, but its Markan, Matthean, Lukan or Johannine form is being heard/read *for the first time*.

Every narrative creates such an implied reader, but it would be a mistake to think that one has performed one's task of interpretation once one has traced the temporal flow of a narrative through the experience of the implied reader. Such a use of literary techniques will still only tell us how an author achieves an effect. It still does not tell us what the text means for the reader *in front of the text*. What must be asked is: in what way does the implied reader *in the text* speak to the knowledge and experience of the real reader *of the text*?

The secret of the lasting value of a narrative lies in the mutuality which is created between the implied reader *in the text* and the real reader *of the text*. When I read a good novel for the first time, I become the implied reader. In a classic, I identify with such a reader. It is the mutuality between the implied reader *in the text* and the real reader *of the text* which makes any given text a classic. As David Tracy has said: 'The classic text's real disclosure is its claim to attention on the ground that an event of understanding proper to finite human beings has here found expression'.[35]

The practice of reading and the community of readers which has produced the Bible is an example of that truth. As we continue to read the Gospels after nearly two thousand years of reading, in a variety of contexts, we can be sure that there has been a mutuality between their implied and real readers.[36] The four 'readings' which follow will trace the beginnings of the implied reader of the four Gospels. The narrative raises problems which the implied reader will solve through the ongoing reading of the story of Jesus. Did these solutions speak to the Marcan, Matthean, Lukan and Johannine communities, the intended reader?[37] They were part of the world of the narrative of the Gospels in a way that the real reader can never be. Do they still speak to real readers at the end of the second millenium?

Narrative critical *theory* rightly distinguishes between an implied reader who emerges from the unfolding

---

35 D. Tracy, *The Analogical Imagination: Christian Theology and the Culture of Pluralism* (New York: Crossroad, 1981) p. 102. See also the study of D. Culbertson, *The Poetics of Revelation. Recognition and the Narrative Tradition* (Studies in American Biblical Hermeneutics 4; Macon: Mercer, 1989).

36 Some contemporary hermeneutical approaches to the Bible would find the word 'mutuality' too friendly. Some liberation and feminist scholars relate hostilely to the implied reader. However, a relationship there must be. On this, see E. Schüssler-Fiorenza, 'The Function of Scripture in the Liberation Struggle. A Critical Feminist Hermeneutics and Liberation Theology', in *Bread not Stone. The Challenge of Feminist Biblical Interpretation* (Boston: Beacon, 1984) pp. 43-63, and especially S.M. Schneiders, *Beyond Patching. Faith and Feminism in the Catholic Church* (Mahwah: Paulist Press, 1991) p. 37-71.

37 Throughout the studies which follow, for the sake of clarity and simplicity, I will refer to the Evangelists by the traditional names of Mark, Matthew, Luke and John, without laying claim to any knowledge as to whom the real authors may have been.

narration, the intended reader, for whom the narrative was originally written (for whom it was originally 'intended' by a real author), and the real reader, whoever, wherever and whenever he or she may take the text in hand. Reading *practice* does not make such neat distinctions. Our experience of reading is that some stories speak to us, while others do not. If, at times, in the lectures that follow, my attempt to trace an emerging implied reader seem to cross all the *theoretical* boundaries between the reader *in* and the many readers *of* the text, this should not be a matter of concern. They who have eyes to read and a heart to respond, let them read and respond!

Indeed, the fact that a series of lectures dedicated to reading Gospel texts can still draw large audiences is an indication that a relationship exists between the implied reader and the real reader. We real readers late in the twentieth century still find that our response, in dialogue with the experience of almost two thousand years of Christian life, often resonates with the unfolding relationship between the implied author and the implied reader in the Gospels. On the other hand we may find (and no doubt many do find) that such a response is fatuous in our real world of men, money and machines. But that is not the only thing that might happen. Sometimes we may have a further response which is independent of the implied reader, and thus outside the control of the author. It is unavoidable that our response, either of empathy or antipathy, will be the result of our privileged position as the recipients of almost 2000 years of the Christian practice of reading the Gospels.[38] As Honoré de Balzac's

---

38 For further reflections along the lines of this paragraph, see R. Morgan – J. Barton, *Biblical Interpretation*, pp. 167-202. See also S. Prickett, *Words and The Word. Language, poetics and biblical interpretation* (Cambridge:

narrator informs his implied reader at the beginning of *Père Goriot*: 'You may be certain that this drama is neither fiction nor romance. *All is true*, so true that everyone can recognise the elements of the tragedy in his own household, in his own heart perhaps'.[39] Or, as J.R.R. Tolkien has reminded us: '*Spell* means both a story told, and a formula of power over living men'.[40]

In my reading of the beginnings of the four Gospels which follow (Mk 1:1-13; Mt 1-2; Lk 1-2; Jn 1:1-18), my aim is to trace the emerging implied reader. Whether or not such a reader's experience matches that of you, the real reader, is beyond my control, as it was beyond the control of the real authors of the Gospels. Two thousand years of Christian history, however, is fair indication that many real readers have 'entered the fictional contract'; they have become the implied reader.[41] Thus, in all that follows, I will generally speak simply of 'the reader'. I do this aware of the theoretical distinction between implied, intended and real readers, but convinced that in a satisfactory reading experience they are one: 'the reader' is born.

CONCLUSION

Over the past 200 years Gospel scholarship has moved encouragingly from a diachronic analysis of the text: its

---

University Press, 1986) pp. 33-36; A.M. Solomon, 'Story upon Story', *Sem* 46 (1989) 3. Unacceptable is the judgment of G. Steiner, *Real Presences*, p. 40: 'The Torah is indeterminately synchronic with all individual and communal life. The Gospels, Epistles and Acts are not'. See pp. 40-45.

39 H. de Balzac, *Old Goriot* (Penguin Classics; Harmondsworth: Penguin Books, 1951) p. 28. See, on this, G. Josipovici, *The Book of God*, pp. 3-28.

40 J.R.R. Tolkien, *Tree and Leaf*, p. 32. The English word 'Gospel' is formed from the Old English 'god-spell'. See Tolkien's reflections upon the Gospel story in *ibid.*, pp. 62-63.

41 See S. Chatman, *Story and Discourse*, p. 150.

previous history, what are the elements which formed the text as we now have it, and what is the history of each of those elements ... into a more synchronic analysis: what response is elicited from the reader of a Gospel narrative.[42] Borrowing language from two of my enduring interests, one could say that our approach to the New Testament has 'changed ends'.[43] While once we concerned ourselves over the situation which gave birth to a certain text, we are now more interested in the response which a narrative elicits from a reader.

But it is important to recognise that each stage in the developing history of Gospel interpretation has depended upon the work already done. There would have been no redaction criticism without the discoveries of the form critics who posed the question of the theological and literary creativity of the early Church. There would have been no literary and narrative criticism without the work of the redaction critics who turned their attention from the individual pericope to the theological perspective of the whole utterance. Thus, while today we attempt to understand and communicate the response which the text is eliciting from its reader, we are unable to do this without first seeing where the text came from.[44]

---

42   The terms 'diachronic' and 'synchronic' come from structuralism. I am using the terms loosely, as do most contemporary New Testament critics.

43   For the uninitiated, in the game of Cricket a bowler can 'change ends', and in Australian Rules Football the teams 'change ends' three times during the course of the game.

44   I am doing a grave injustice, in this survey, by omitting a more detailed description of two other contemporary approaches to the New Testament. Social-science perspectives are sometimes used to discover in the texts the distinctive social relationships of the communities which produced them. For a survey, see B.J. Malina, *The New Testament World: Insights from Cultural Anthropology* (Atlanta: John Knox, 1981). Two important studies emerging from this approach are: W. Meeks, *The First Urban Christians:*

Over the centuries different ecclesiastical traditions have tended to appropriate the *world in the text* to defend practices and support dogmas which had little or no basis in the text itself. Form criticism and redaction criticism healthily questioned this widespread practice. These earlier, more historical, approaches to the texts of the Gospels forced the preachers and the Churches to pay more attention to the *world behind the text*. It is not enough simply to ask what a biblical text means for me today. We have been made aware of the need to ask what the text originally meant. This can be ascertained by means of the historical methods developed by the form and redaction critics.[45] But the *world in front of the text*, the reader and the listener, also has a critical role to play in the interpretation of the Bible.[46] But have we now come full-circle? Will these new approaches lead us back to the old fundamentalism, a new form of subjectivism where I read myself into the text? This is a real danger, and it can only be avoided by developing a dialogue across all three worlds: the world behind, in and in front of the text. On the horizon where these worlds meet, justice will be done in the contemporary reading of an ancient text.[47]

The Social World of the Apostle Paul (New Haven: Yale University Press, 1983) and J.H. Neyrey, *An Ideology of Revolt. John's Christology in Social Science Perspective* (Philadelphia: Fortress, 1989). Postmodern exegesis attempts to destabilise the biblical interpretation by detaching the texts from any pre-discoursed reality. See especially S.D. Moore, *Literary Criticism*, pp. 108-170. See also G.A. Phillips, 'Exegesis as Critical Praxis: Reclaiming History and Text from a Postmodern Perspective', *Sem* 51 (1990) 7-49; F.W. Burnett, 'Postmodern Biblical Exegesis: The Eve of Historical Criticism', *Sem* 51 (1990) 51-80.

45 On this, see J.A. Fitzmyer, 'Historical Criticism', pp. 244-259.

46 On this, see the important essay of A.J. Kelly, 'The Historical Jesus and Human Subjectivity: A Response to John Meier', *Pac* 4 (1991) 202-228.

47 On this, see A.N. Wilder, *The Bible and the Literary Critic* (Minneapolis: Fortress Press, 1991). With the exception of the reminiscences on pp. 51-72,

For almost 2000 years the Christian Churches have deepened the understanding of their faith and developed their Christian practice with the Gospels in hand. As we approach the third millenium, after almost 200 years of critical Gospel scholarship, have we, the Christian Churches, witnesses and ministers of the Word, recovered from the shock of Reimarus, Strauss and Baur? I wonder.

Form and redaction critics have shown that the Gospels came into existence as written texts to address the pastoral problems which faced the early Church. But why do we still read these same texts? Simply because of the Church's authoritative placing of them in the Canon as 'inspired books'? Behind the issues of the Canon and inspiration lies the lived experience of the Church, that certain documents addressed the human predicament in a perennially significant fashion, while other documents simply came and went. In narrative critical terms, the response elicited from the reader *in* the narrative has resonated with the response elicited, over the centuries, from the many real readers *of* those narratives.[48]

The shock of Reimarus must be overcome. As the Christian Church proclaims the Word of God, accepted as such from our past, it has a duty to focus its proclamation upon the human predicament perennially addressed by that Word. I submit that it is to the detriment of the theological, ministerial and pastoral endeavour of the Christian Church that New Testament scholars be kept in their playpen.

the whole book argues this case, but see esp. pp. 132-148. See also M.A. Powell, *What is Narrative Criticism?*, pp. 85-101.
48 See M.A. Powell, *What is Narrative Criticism?*, pp. 98-101.

2 BEGINNING THE GOSPEL OF MARK
MARK 1:1-13

Already in antiquity certain conventions had been established for the beginning of a story.[1] It had already been recognised that 'placing an item at the beginning or at the end may radically change the process of reading as well as the final product'.[2] Among the four Gospels this is particularly evident at the beginning of the Gospel of Luke (see Lk 1:1-4),[3] but all the Gospels have a recognisable 'beginning'. Beginnings influence the process of reading the Good News of Mark, Matthew, Luke and John.

---

1   See the survey of D.E. Smith, 'Narrative Beginnings in Ancient Literature and Theory', *Sem* 52 (1991) 1-9.
2   S. Rimmon-Kenan, *Narrative Fiction: Contemporary Poetics* (New Accents: London/ New York: Methuen, 1983) p. 120. See also M.C. Parsons, 'Reading a Beginning', pp. 18-21. On this feature in narrative, see M. Sternberg, *Expositional Modes and Temporal Ordering in Fiction* (Baltimore: John Hopkins University Press, 1978); G. Watson, 'The Sense of a Beginning', *Sewanee Review* 86 (1978) 539-548; V. Brombert, 'Opening Signals in Narrative', *New Literary History* 10 (1979) 489-502; R. Pope, 'Beginnings', *The Georgia Review* 36 (1982) 733-751.
3   See H.J. Cadbury, *The Making of Luke-Acts* (London: SPCK, 1958³) pp. 203-209, and the parallels from antiquity cited there. See D.E. Smith, 'Narrative Beginnings', pp. 1-2.

WHERE DOES THE BEGINNING END?[4]

Most contemporary scholars have claimed that one should see Mark 1:1-15, rather than 1:1-13, as the prologue to the Gospel of Mark.[5] There can be little doubt that vv. 14-15 contain a summary which is programmatic and which has verbal link with v. 1 (especially *evangelion*), but I regard it as an introduction to the first narrative section of the Gospel which, for reasons which will emerge, comes to a climax in v. 13: 'He was with the wild beasts'.

I read 1:14-3:6 as a deliberately designed narrative which reports on Jesus' encounter with Israel, beginning with a summary (1:14-15) and the vocation of the disciples (1:16-20), at the end of which a decision is made by representatives of Israel: 'The Pharisees went out and immediately held counsel with the Herodians against him, how to destroy him' (3:6). This is followed by 3:7-6:6a, beginning with a summary (3:7-12) and the institution of the Twelve (3:13-19), reporting Jesus' establishment of a new family. It leads to the decision from the inhabitants of 'his own country' (6:1) who know his Mother and brothers and sisters; 'And they took offence at him' (6:3). In a third section, running from 6:6b to 8:29, beginning with a summary (6:6b) and the account of Jesus' sending out of the disciples (6:7-30), the narrator reports Jesus' growing

---

4   On the importance of this question, see E. S. Malbon, 'Ending at the Beginning: A Response', *Sem* 52 (1990) 176.
5   See, for example, L. Keck, 'The Introduction to Mark's Gospel', NTS 12 (1965-66) 352-370; W. Grundmann, *Das Evangelium nach Markus* (THZNT 2; Berlin: Evangelische Verlagsanstalt, 1973⁶) p. 34; H. Anderson, *The Gospel of Mark* (NCB; London: Oliphants, 1976) pp. 62-65; R. Pesch, *Das Markusevangelium* (HTKNT II/1; Freiburg: Herder, 1977²) pp. 71-73; J. Drury, 'Mark', in A. Alter – F. Kermode (eds.), *The Literary Guide to the Bible* (London: Collins, 1987) pp. 407-409; R.A. Guelich, *Mark 1-8:26* (WBC; Dallas: Word Books, 1989) pp. 1-5; M.E. Boring, 'Mark 1:1-15 and the Beginning of the Gospel', *Sem* 52 (1990) 55-59.

revelation of himself to his disciples, culminating with the confession of Peter: 'You are the Christ' (8:29).[6]

Thus, on three occasions in the first half of the Gospel, the reader will encounter summary statements (see 1:14-15; 3:7-12; 6:6b) which are followed immediately by material which deals with Jesus' calling and missioning disciples (see 1:16-20; 3:13-20; 6:7-30). Each narrative 'block' which begins in this way concludes with some form of decision: he must die (3:6), his townsfolk will not believe in him (6:1-6a), he is the Christ (8:29).[7] Despite the close links which can be made between vv. 1-13 and vv. 14-15,[8] the imperatives of v. 15 (repent, believe) cause the reader to look forward, wondering whether a response to such commands will show how the coming of the kingdom *(basileia)* and the good news *(evangelion)* affects the human story.

6 The central section of Mark's narrative is formed by a bridge. The first half of the story closes at 8:29, but something else is happening between 8:22-26 and 10:46-52 where two stories of blind men who come to sight are told. For some further reflections on 8:22-10:52, see F.J. Moloney, *The Living Voice of the Gospel. The Gospels Today* (Melbourne: Collins Dove, 1987) pp. 43-63. For a similar view, see M.E. Boring, 'Mark 1:1-15', pp. 43-46.

7 For this narrative shape, see E. Schweizer, 'Mark's Theological Achievement', in W. Telford (ed.), *The Interpretation of Mark* (IRT 7; London/Philadelphia: SPCK/Fortress, 1985) pp. 57-58; X. Léon-Dufour, 'L'Evangile selon saint Marc', in A. George – P. Grelot (eds.), *Introduction à la Bible* (7 vols.; Paris: Desclée, 1976) vol. 2, pp. 48-50. The use of summary coupled with discipleship material is sometimes seen as structurally important only as far as 3:7-20. See, for example, V. Taylor, *The Gospel According to St. Mark* (London: Macmillan, 1966²) pp. 107-108, and W.L. Lane, *Commentary on the Gospel of Mark* (NICNT; Grand Rapids: Eerdmans, 1974) pp. 29-30. H. Baarlink, *Anfängliches Evangelium. Ein Beitrag zur näheren Bistimmung der theologischen Motive im Markusevangelium* (Kampen: J.H. Kok, 1977) pp. 73-78, offers a survey of 27 different outlines of Mark.

8 See, for example, the possible inclusion indicated by the use of *evangelion* in v. 1 and v. 15. See further, R. Pesch, *Markusevangelium*, p. 72; J. Drury, 'Mark', pp. 407-408. C. Myers, *Binding the Strong Man. A Political Reading of Mark's Story of Jesus* (Maryknoll: Orbis, 1988) p. 122, rightly calls vv. 1-15 a 'narrative of succession (Isaiah-John-Jesus-Kingdom)'. He fails to recognise, however, that God speaks in vv. 2-3, not Isaiah. See also pp. 124-126, where vv. 2-3 are discussed.

The two-fold use of *evangelion* in vv. 14-15 does not look back to v. 1, but forward into Jesus' life, ministry and death as the fulfilment of time and the presence of the Kingdom.

The reading of vv. 1-13 which follows must test this hypothesis further. Does the reader rise satisfied from the experience of the narrative down to v. 13? If not, what lies at the root of the reader's dissatisfaction? Would a reading of vv. 14-15 resolve it? I am suggesting, even at this early stage, that vv. 1-13 will inform the reader, but also create a desire to read on. As Shlomith Rimmon-Kenan has remarked: 'Narrative texts implicitly keep promising the reader the great prize of understanding — later'.[9]

THE SHAPE OF THE NARRATIVE

There is widespread agreement among commentators, critical editions and modern translations, that Mark 1:1-13 is made up of a superscription to the Gospel (v. 1), a description of the Baptist and his activity (vv. 2-8), the baptism of Jesus (vv. 9-11) and Jesus' temptation (vv. 12-13).[10] Adopting more literary criteria, one must identify such features as a change of character and action,

---

9 S. Rimmon-Kenan, *Narrative Fiction*, p. 125. Against M.E. Boring, 'Mark 1:1-15', pp. 58-59, who claims that v. 13 is still incomplete, and needs vv. 14-15 for 'cohesiveness'.

10 See, for example, V. Taylor, *St Mark*, pp. 151-164; W. Grundmann, *Markus*, pp. 25-35; W.L. Lane, *Mark*, pp. 41-62; H. Anderson, *Mark*, pp. 65-83; W. Harrington, *Mark* (NTM 4; Wilmington: Michael Glazier, 1979) pp. 2-8; M. D. Hooker, *The Message of Mark* (London: Epworth, 1983) pp. 7-8; UBSGNT; JB; NJB; TOB. M.E. Boring, 'Mark 1:1-15', pp. 59-61 modifies this by focusing his attention on the characters. He suggests v. 1: title; vv. 2-8: John, identified by an off-stage voice (v. 2-4), active (vv. 5-6), preaching repentance in terms of promise (vv. 7-8); vv. 9-15: Jesus, identified by an off-stage voice (vv. 9-11), active (vv. 12-13), preaching repentance in terms of fulfillment (vv. 14-15). This structure pays too little attention to the main actor (vigorously seen as such by Boring himself [see pp. 61-63]): God.

the focalisation of the narrative,[11] the agent in the action described and changes of time and place. A close reading of the text along these lines suggests that there are five elements in the narrative shape of Mark 1:1-13.

1. **vv. 1-3:** Behind the first words of the Gospel of Mark stands the God of the narrator. The reader is led through a series of claims. He is told that he is at the beginning of a story *(archê)* which is good news. It is about a man called Jesus who is the Christ. All of this is true, claims the narrator, because he is the Son *of God*.[12] Further proof for this astounding opening claim is added by using the words of the prophet Isaiah (vv. 2-3). Words *of God* enter the story, in direct speech, using the first person singular, addressing a listener in the second person singular, telling him that he will send a messenger to prepare his way. The messenger prepares the way of 'the Lord'. The first character to play an active role in the Gospel of Mark is God, describing his sent one as 'the Lord'.

2. **vv. 4-6:** The narrator tells his reader that God's word is partially fulfilled. The promised forerunner of vv. 2-3 appears in the narrative. At this stage he plays no active role. The narrator merely reports his arrival on the scene, his appearance, activity and behaviour: a prophetic messenger, sent to prepare the way.

---

11 Focalisation pays attention to the eyes through which the reported events are seen. On this, see G. Genette, *Narrative Discourse*, pp. 189-211 and Idem, *Revisited*, pp. 72-78. See also S. Rimmon-Kenan, *Narrative Fiction*, pp. 71-85.

12 Accepting the reading *huiou theou* in v. 1 (against, for example, R. Pesch, *Markusevangelium*, pp. 74, 77). See also M.-J. Lagrange, *Evangile selon Saint Marc* (EB; Paris: Gabalda, 1920) p. 3; V. Taylor, *Mark*, p. 152; For a full discussion, see C.R. Kazmierski, *Jesus, the Son of God. A Study of the Marcan Tradition and its Redaction by the Evangelist* (FzB 33; Würzburg: Echter, 1979) pp. 1-9.

3. **vv. 7-8:** God's word is further fulfilled as the figure of the Baptist actively enters the story, witnessing *in direct speech* to the one who is coming. The narrative is focused upon him as he announces the coming one as 'the Stronger one', one before whom he is most unworthy, one who 'will baptise with the Holy Spirit'. Not only is he preparing the way, but he is preparing the way for 'the Lord'.

4. **vv. 9-11:** The focalisation of the narrative returns to the narrator. Jesus enters, but only through the narration. He himself does nothing. Things happen to him: he is baptised by John, the Spirit descends upon him and a voice from heaven describes him. The use of the passive verbs and the final intervention of the voice from above keeps God at the centre of the action, even though he is never named.

5. **vv. 12-13:** The central character in this brief narrative is still Jesus, and the narrator is still responsible for the story. However, the scene shifts from the river Jordan to the desert. On the whole, things still happen to Jesus: the Spirit drives him into the desert, he is tempted by Satan and ministered to by angels. However, for the first time in the story, Jesus is described as significantly active: 'he was with the wild beasts'. As the prologue draws to a close, Jesus takes over from God as the active agent in the story.

God dominates most of the prologue. God is mentioned by name in v. 1, and present in his word in vv. 2-3. In vv. 4-5 and 6-8 the Baptist is the subject of most of the verbs, but his activity is the fulfilment of the word of God in vv. 2-3. He points away from himself and eventually fades from the narrative as Jesus from Nazareth is introduced as a third person figure. God and his Spirit are the main actors in Jesus' first experiences until, at the close of the narrative Jesus is *with* the wild beasts and served by the angels.[13]

This preliminary description of the shape of Mark 1:1-13 enables us to present a structured reading of the text itself as follows:

Mark 1:1-13

[1] The beginning of the good news of Jesus Christ, the Son of God.
[2] As it is written in Isaiah the prophet, 'Behold I send my messenger before thy face, who shall prepare thy way;
[3] the voice of one crying in the wilderness: Prepare the way of the Lord, make his paths straight'.

*God's words ('I')
confirm
the narrator's
program for
Jesus ('thy'):
'My messenger'
'The Lord'*

---

[4] John the baptiser appeared in the wilderness, preaching a baptism of repentance for the forgiveness of sins.
[5] And there went out to him all the country of Judea, and all the people of Jerusalem; and they were baptised by him in the river of Jordan, confessing their sins.
[6] Now John was clothed with camel's hair, and had a leather girdle around his waist, and ate locusts and wild honey.

*Part-fulfilment
of God's words is
narrated:
The Precursor*

---

[7] And he preached, saying, 'After me comes one who is mightier than I, the thong of whose sandals I am not worthy to stoop down and untie. **[8]** I have baptised you with water; but he will baptise you with the Holy Spirit.

Fulfilment promised. The Precursor announces: The Mightier One with the Spirit.

---

[9] In those days Jesus came from Nazareth of Galilee and was baptised by John in the Jordan. **[10]** And when he came up out of the water, immediately he saw the heavens opened and the Spirit descending upon him like a dove; **[11]** and a voice came from heaven, 'Thou art my beloved Son; with thee I am well pleased'.

Narration of events which happen to Jesus via the Baptist and God.

---

[12] The Spirit immediately drove him out into the wilderness. **[13]** And he was in the wilderness forty days, tempted by Satan; and he was with the wild beasts; and the angels ministered to him.

Narration of events where Jesus acts in the spirit.

READING THE NARRATIVE

1. Reading Mark vv. 1-3

The first word the reader encounters echoes the first words of Genesis: 'the beginning' *(hê archê)*.[14] It also simply

---

14 See especially E. Lohmeyer, *Das Evangelium des Markus* (Meyer Kommentar 2; Göttingen: Vandenhoeck und Ruprecht, 1967[17]) p. 10.

indicates the first word of a long story. Both meanings are involved. The Markan narrative 'begins' with an echo of God's original creation.[15] Although its location in the narrative recalls Genesis, the reader is not presented with any further creation themes. It is rather the beginning of 'the good news' *(tou euangeliou)*, and a man's name, Jesus, is immediately introduced into the story.[16] The reader is familiar with the expression 'good news'. It is found both in the Greek translation of the Old Testament (the LXX) and the Hellenistic world. In the LXX Isaiah used it to proclaim the 'good news' of God's rule, salvation or vindication (see LXX Is 40:9; 41:27; 52:7; 60:6; 61:1), while the Greek writers used it to announce a royal birth, a military victory or a political triumph.[17] The newness about the expression in Mark 1:1 is its use as a noun. It is not a proclamation of good news, it is the good news itself which is beginning.[18] The reader next discovers that it is good news about a man.

The good news is: Jesus is the Christ.[19] Although the two expressions, Jesus and Christ had become a proper

---

15 See H. Anderson, *Mark*, p. 66.

16 M.E. Boring, 'Mark 1:1-15', pp. 47-53, has persuasively argued the case for *archê* as the beginning of the whole utterance, and further suggested that it may mean more than 'beginning'. The *evangelion* of Jesus which follows is also 'the beginning and foundation for the church's contemporary preaching' (p. 53).

17 C. Myers, *Binding*, pp. 122-124, interestingly suggests that 'Mark is taking dead aim at Caesar and his legitimating myths ... It is a declaration of war upon the political culture of the empire'. He pays no attention to the use of the verb in the LXX.

18 Both in the LXX and in Hellenistic documents, the verbal form *euangelizomai* is mostly found. Paul uses the noun to speak of his 'gospel' message of God's victory won in the death and resurrection of Jesus Christ. For summaries, see C.E.B. Cranfield, *The Gospel according to St Mark* (CGTC; Cambridge: University Press, 1959) pp. 35-36; R.A. Guelich, *Mark*, pp. 13-14. The implied reader of Mark's Gospel cannot be credited with a knowledge of the Pauline use of the noun.

19 I am reading an objective genitive here: 'the good news concerning Jesus Christ'. Many read it as subjective, 'the Gospel proclaimed by Jesus Christ'. For the discussion and bibliography, see R.A. Guelich, *Mark*, p. 9.

name by this stage in the early Church's preaching,[20] the reader first meets a proper name, Jesus, and then an attribute, Christ.[21] The good news is that the man Jesus is the Messiah, but he is more: he is the son of God. The reader understands this final expression in close association with 'Christ'. However important the notion of Jesus as 'the son' might be for the Markan Christology (see further 1:11; 3:11; 5:7; 9:7; 14:61; 15:39), at this stage of the reading experience the expression merely clarifies for the reader the way in which the man Jesus is the Christ.[22] Like the ideal King of Israel (see 2 Sam 7:14; Ps 2:7; 89:26-29) and the chosen People of Israel (see Ex 4:22; Is 63:16; Hos 11:1), he can be regarded 'son of God', and thus Messiah,[23] because of his relationship with God.[24]

The reader has begun to read the good news that Jesus is the Christ, but is immediately aware that such news

---

20 Already in Paul Jesus Christ is widely used as a proper name. For a critical survey, see W. Kramer, *Christ, Lord, Son of God* (SBT 50; London: SCM, 1966) pp. 203-214.

21 See, for this position, C.E.B. Cranfield, *St Mark*, pp. 37-38; R.A. Guelich, *Mark*, pp. 9-10.

22 Thus, the textual problem cannot be solved by simply claiming that it has been added by a later scribe in the light of the importance of the Son of God Christology of the Gospel. See, for example, R. Pesch, *Markusevangelium*, p. 77. It plays an important narrative role as the final affirmation of the first sentence which the reader reads, without any reference to the rest of the Gospel.

23 See the first century messianic use of 2 Sam 7 in 4QFlorilegium I:10-13. This same fragment also associates Ps 2 with the end time. See I:18-II:4.

24 Against, for example, E. Lohmeyer, *Markus*, p. 4 and W.L. Lane, *Mark*, pp. 44-45, who see 'son of God' here as 'altogether supernatural' (Lane, *Mark*, p. 44, note 23). See the comprehensive treatment of the use of 'son of God' in Judaism in B.J. Byrne, *'Sons of God – Seed of Abraham'. A Study of the Idea of the Sonship of God of All Christians in Paul against the Jewish Background* (AnBib 83; Rome: Biblical Institute Press, 1979) pp. 9-78. See esp. pp. 16-18 and 59-62.

depends upon God. God is the main character in the narrative as the narrator introduces prophecy with the use of the divine passive: 'As it has been written' *(kathôs gegraptai)*. The use of the perfect passive informs the reader that God is the active agent in the writing of this word by the prophet, Isaiah.[25] Secondly, while the prophet Isaiah may have been the spokesman, the word of God spoken in the past is still effective in the present.

In direct speech God speaks as 'I' to a 'you'. He announces that a messenger will precede the coming of the one addressed. Reporting the direct speech of the messenger, the one addressed in v. 2b (Mal 3:1) becomes *the Lord* in v. 3b (Is 40:3). A messenger will cry in the wilderness: prepare the way of the *kyrios* (v. 3). Whatever the proper name of the second person singular ('you') may be in v. 2b, the reader now knows that he will be 'the Lord' (v. 3b). The author's combination of Malachi and Isaiah as the words of God to begin his narrative transforms them from their original context. Here it is God who witnesses to a coming one, and he names him *ho kyrios*. This expression is used systematically in the LXX to translate YHWH, the sacred name for God.[26] God names a figure yet to appear in the story, by his own name.[27]

---

25 The citation in vv. 2-3, in fact, is composite. v. 2 comes from Mal 3:1 and Ex 23:20, while v. 3 is from Is 40:3. 'This is the only place in the Gospel where Mark himself (as distinct from the characters in the story) appeals to the Old Testament, and he manages to get his reference wrong!' (M.D. Hooker, *Message*, p. 4). This has created textual difficulties in v. 2. Many copyists alter 'in Isaiah the prophet' to 'in the prophets'. See B.M. Metzger, *A Textual Commentary on the Greek New Testament* (London/New York: United Bible Socieites, 1971) p. 73.

26 See G. Quell, Art. *kyrios ktl.*', in *TDNT* 3 (1965) 1058-1081; C.E.B. Cranfield, *St Mark*, pp. 39-40.

27 See H.C. Waetjen, *A Reordering of Power. A Socio-Political Reading of Mark's Gospel* (Minneapolis: Fortress Press, 1989) pp. 64-65.

The introduction of the future tense of the verb to describe the task of the messenger, 'who shall prepare thy way' (v. 2), brings narrative time into the story time. The narrator has broken into the regular succession of events along the time line of the story (story time), to point to some time in the future, not yet a part of the reader's experience but important for some future point in the unfolding narrative (narrative time).[28] Involved in this future orientation of the narrative is also the figure identified in the direct speech of God as 'the Lord'. At this stage of the narrative the reader only knows of the central importance of God for the good news about Jesus the Messiah, and his design that a messenger will prepare the way of the Lord.[29] The reader is led to suspect that Jesus, the Messiah and the son (v. 1), is also 'the Lord' (v. 3). This remarkable suggestion must be verified by reading further.

2. Reading Mark vv. 4-6

There is disappointment in store for the reader, as the fulfilment of the lesser promise of the word of God (vv. 2-3) is described. The narrator tells of the messenger, rather than 'the Lord'. What had been promised 'happens': John

---

28 Story time is the reporting of a regular succession of events along an or- dered time-line. An author can break out of story time into narrative time either to look forward, called a *prolepsis*, or backwards, called an *analepsis*. For the classical study of this feature of narrative, and for the terminology just mentioned, see G. Genette, *Narrative Discourse*, pp. 33-38. See also S. Rimmon-Kenan, *Narrative Fiction*, pp. 43-58. For a reading of Mark from this perspective, see N.R. Petersen, *Literary Criticism for New Testa- ment Critics* (GBSNT; Philadelphia: Fortress, 1978) pp. 49-80.

29 This is not only way in which the 'I – messenger – you' can be interpreted. For the various possibilities, see C. Myers, *Binding*, pp. 124-125.

the baptiser appeared *(egeneto)* in the desert. The reader may not have any knowledge of this figure, but he is the one spoken of by God. The narrator picks up the words of God which promised 'the voice of one crying *in the wilderness*' (v. 3a) and John the baptiser who 'appeared *in the wilderness*' (v. 4a).[30]

His mission of preaching a baptism of repentance reminds the reader of the prophets' call for a whole-hearted return to YHWH (see, for example, Jer 18:11; Is 55:7; Zech 1:4) through a 'turning back' towards Israel's unique God.[31] The precise nature of the practice of John's baptism is hard to determine, but it is understood by the reader alongside Pharisaic, proselyte and Qumran baptismal practices.[32] It is an external sign of a serious commitment to 'turning back' to God. The effectiveness of John's preaching is enhanced by the somewhat exaggerated claims that 'all the country of Judea and all the country of Jerusalem' went out to him at the Jordan river.[33] Whatever reservations a reader may have concerning the precise details of this report, the author makes his point: John made a great impression.[34]

---

30 The 'wilderness' appears three times in vv. 1-13 (see vv. 3, 4 and 12). It ties the prologue together as a literary unit, and has both a positive (see vv. 3-4) and an ambiguous (see v. 12) role in the narrative.

31 The Greek *metanoein* translates the Hebrew *shûb*, which means to 'turn back' or 'return'. On this, see C.E.B. Cranfield, *St Mark*, pp. 43-46.

32 On this, see W. Michaelis, 'Zum jüdischen Hintergrund der Johannestaufe' *Jud* 7 (1951) 81-120; J. Gnilka, 'Die essenischen Tauchbäder und die Johannestaufe', *RevQ* 3 (1961) 185-207.

33 For a generally convincing study of the historical background to the Baptist material in the Gospel, see J. Murphy-O'Connor, 'John the Baptist and Jesus: History and Hypotheses', *NTS* 36 (1990) 359-374.

34 There is no need to contrast the many Judeans of v. 5 and the solitary Galilean of v. 9, as does E. Lohmeyer, *Markus*, p. 20.

Consequently, many acknowledged their sins as they turned back to God. However, the reader is better informed than those who flock to the Baptist. The reader has heard the words of God himself (vv. 2-3) and is aware that this is only the messenger. The mission of the Baptist is both directed by God and oriented towards God. Something more is yet to be narrated.

The reader's awareness of the central role of God in the narrative is further strengthened by the brief description of the Baptist's appearance and diet. There have been many who have associated this description with the description of Elijah in 2 Kings 1:8.[35] Such an interpretation is largely coloured by Jesus' words later in the Gospel which identify the Baptist with Elijah (see 9:11-13), but such information is yet to be given to the reader.[36] The description of his dress is nothing more than 'the nomadic attire of the wilderness in general and ... the prophetic dress in particular'.[37] The same must be said for his form of nourishment. He lives as an ascetic, neither eating meat nor drinking wine. While this note finds its parallel in other synoptic descriptions of John the Baptist as one who comes neither eating nor drinking (Mt 11:18//Lk 7:33), such behaviour is typical of late Jewish prophets.[38] The Baptist belongs to a long line as one of God's prophets. This indicates to the reader that he is what he is because of God.

---

35 See, for example, V. Taylor, St Mark, p. 156; W. Crundmann, Markus, p. 28; R. Pesch, Markusevangelium, p. 81; M.D. Hooker, Message, p. 9; H.C. Waetjen, Reordering, pp. 65-66; C. Myers, Binding, pp. 126-127.

36 See W.L. Lane, Mark, p. 51.

37 R.A. Guelich, Mark, p. 21.

38 See, for example, Dan 1:8; The Lives of the Prophets 4:14; Martyrdom of Isaiah 2:10-11. For the non-biblical texts, see J.H. Charlesworth (ed.), The Old Testament Pseudepigrapha (2 vols.; London: Darton, Longman & Todd, 1985) vol. 2, pp. 390, 158.

3. Reading Mark vv. 7-8

A new element is added to the story in vv. 7-8. The direct speech of John the Baptist's proclamation (the technical word *kerussein* is used) is somewhat at variance with the reader's expectation of a prophet of YHWH, who traditionally recalled YHWH's *past* saving interventions. The Baptist does not call the people back to the traditional ways of Israel. Fulfilling God's promise of v. 3: 'the voice of one crying in the wilderness', the Baptist points *forward* to the future coming of 'the mightier one' *(ho ischuroteros).*[39] While the term may not summon up directly messianic claims, the reader is aware that God has been called 'the Mightier one' (see 2 Sam 22:31; 23:5; Ps 7:12; Is 49:25. See also Is 9:6). The reader's attention is being shifted from the God who sends the Baptist to the mightier one who will come after the Baptist. As in v. 3b, where God spoke of the coming one as 'the Lord' *(ho kyrios),* so also here an expression from the LXX used to speak of God 'the Mightier one' *(ho ischuroteros)* is applied by the Baptist to the one who will come after him. Before the character appears in the narrative, the reader is already asking the question: is YHWH's unique role as *kyrios* and *ischuroteros* being shifted to the coming one?

The reader may hold the Baptist in high esteem.[40] After all, he is the messenger of God who is sent to

---

39 The Baptist's indication that the Mightier one is coming 'after me' could have either a local or a temporal sense. See BAGD, p. 575. If the former, it could indicate that Jesus came from among his disciples (which was probably the case historically). See W.L. Lane, *Mark*, p. 52; R. Pesch, *Markusevangelium*, p. 83. My reading, insisting on the whole of vv. 7-8 as a prolepsis, regards it as having a purely temporal meaning. See S. Seesemann, Art. *'opisô ktl.'*, *TDNT* 5 (1967) 290.

40 It is often asked whether the Baptist material in the Gospels arose within the context of the early Church's need to assert his inferiority to Jesus.

proclaim the coming of the Lord. The gulf that separates him from the one he announces is indicated by the words of the Baptist who states that he is not even worthy to perform the function of a slave.[41] Jewish sources insist, however, that untying the master's sandals was the one demeaning task never required of a Hebrew servant (see *Mekilta* 21:2; *bKetuboth* 96a). 'To be unworthy of such a task would be to lower oneself below the status of a slave'.[42]

The final words from the Baptist break into story time by both looking *backwards* to his baptising ministry: 'I have baptised (aorist) you with water' and *forward* to the future activity of Jesus: 'He will baptise (future) you with the Holy Spirit'. The juxtaposition of the analepsis and the prolepsis places the reader in a narrative tension between what has been given through the ministry of the Baptist and what will be given by the coming one. The nature of the Baptist's ministry has already been explained to the reader in vv.4-5. The reader is not entirely without background to the notion of a baptism with the Spirit. The prophet Ezekiel had promised, in the name of YHWH:

> I will sprinkle clean water upon you, and you shall be clean from all your uncleannesses, ... A new heart I will give you, and a new spirit I will put within you; ... And I will put my spirit within you, and cause you to walk in my statutes' (Ezek 36:25-27).

No doubt there would have been a need to understand how they related to one another, and much of this material may have had its origins in those discussions. But they need not be the result of polemical clashes between Baptist followers and Jesus followers, as is sometimes claimed.

41 For Jewish background to this task see Str-B Vol. I, p. 121; Vol. II, p. 1.

42 R.A. Guelich, *Mark*, p. 24.

The Qumran sectarians and later Judaism spoke of a spirit-baptism in which the Spirit was a gift of God to his faithful ones; through which his promises for them would be realised.[43] The reader looks forward to the fulfilment of yet another gift of God for which the Baptist's call to repentance has prepared 'all the country of Judea and all the people of Jerusalem' (v. 5). However, the Lord (v. 3), the Mightier one who comes after the Baptist (v. 7) will be the dispenser of the Holy Spirit (v. 8). Not only the names given to God are to be taken over by the coming one, but also one of God's functions as the giver of the Spirit.

Until now Jesus the Christ, the son of God (v. 1) has not appeared in the narrative. God has been the main actor, in his word (vv. 1-3) and through his messenger (vv. 4-6; 7-9). Only in the final stages of the prologue does Jesus appear on the scene.

4. Reading Mark vv. 9-11

The reader encounters a solemn expression which reminds him of important moments in the Old Testament. The NRSV's 'In those days Jesus came' hardly captures the Greek rendition of the Semitic idiom: *kai egeneto en ekeinais tais hêmerais êlthen Iêsous.* Jesus has entered the story. He needs no introduction, as the reader has already been given his name, and has been informed that he is the Christ, the son of God in v. 1. In v. 9, however, such heady claims are absent. His origins are situated in a little

---

43 See 1QS 3:7-9; 4:20-21; 1QH 16:11-12; *The Testament of Levi* 18:6-7 (J.H. Charlesworth, *Pseudepigrapha*, Vol. 1, p. 795). See the helpful discussion of this question in R.A. Guelich, *Mark*, pp. 24-26.

known village, Nazareth, which, for identification, needs to be further described as 'of Galilee'.[44]

The reader waits for some action from this Christ and son of God, but the Baptist is still the main agent as Jesus 'was baptised by John in the Jordan'. By means of the passive verb the author is able to present Jesus as receptive to the ministry of John the Baptist. The main agents in the narrative so far have been God and John the Baptist. This continues, but the Baptist is soon to be elided from the narrative. He baptises Jesus by immersing him in the river Jordan, but as Jesus comes up (v. 10a: *anabainôn*) from the water, a series of events are reported during which divine signs *come down* (v. 10b: *katabainon*) upon him.[45] Jesus has a vision: 'He saw heaven opened and the Spirit descending upon him like a dove'.[46]

In a world where God abides above the firmament and the human story takes place below it, the opening of the heavens indicates that some sort of communication from above to below is about to take place (see Gen 7:11; Is 24:18; 64:1; Ezek 1:1; Rev 4:1; 11:19).[47] After allowing his messenger to play out his role in vv. 4-8, God re-enters the action, as the Baptist disappears. The narrative is reported through the eyes of Jesus, but always as a passive, receptive agent. The Spirit descending upon Jesus fulfils the promises of the gift of the Spirit in the new creation, especially as they are found in the prophet Isaiah (see esp. Is 42:1-5, but also 11:1-3; 61:1; 63:10-14).

44 See C. Myers, *Binding*, p. 128: 'tantamount to introducing him as "Jesus from Nowheresville"'.
45 See J. Drury, 'Mark', p. 408.
46 The absence of proper names in v. 10 makes it difficult to determine who is the subject of 'saw'. Grammatically, however, it must be the subject of v. 9 and the one addressed in v. 11: Jesus.
47 See C.E.B. Cranfield, *St Mark*, p. 53; M.D. Hooker, *Message*, p. 11.

The reader recalls that the creation theme was passingly adumbrated in v. 1. The Gospel began with the same word as Gen 1:1. There the Spirit of God was moving over the face of the waters (v. 3). The Spirit of God now descends upon Jesus 'like a dove'. Despite the widespread use of the symbol of the dove in ancient literature,[48] and its subsequent use in Christian symbolism, there is no precedent for the Markan link between the Spirit and a dove. The reader reads the imagery without any symbolic application. The creating Spirit of God who cannot be *seen*, known to the reader from Genesis and Isaiah, gently descends upon Jesus in the form of a dove, which Jesus can see.[49] The word of God (vv. 1-3) pointed the reader towards Jesus as Christ, son of God and Lord. The ministry of the Baptist (vv. 7-8) promised the coming of the Stronger one who would baptise with the Holy Spirit. Jesus from Nazareth has now been gifted with the Spirit.[50]

---

48 See especially F.L. Lentzen-Deis, *Die Taufe Jesus nach den Synoptikern. Literarkritische und Gattungsgeschichtliche Untersuchungen* (FThSt 4; Frankfurt: Josef Knecht, 1970) pp. 170-183. I am tempted by the suggestions of W.L. Lane, *Mark*, pp. 56-57 and M.D. Hooker, *Message*, pp. 11-12, who looked to Jewish literature (esp. *bHagigah* 15a) for evidence that the Spirit of God in Gen 1:3 is compared to a dove. The evidence, however, is slight and perhaps too late. There may be a link with the use of a dove by Noah in Gen 8:8-12. This was first suggested to be by Antony Campbell, S.J., but is also argued by H.C. Waetjen, *Reordering*, p. 70.

49 Some scholars attempt to resolve the difficulty by reading *hôs peristeran* adverbially: 'The Spirit, coming down as a dove does'. See, for example, L.E. Keck, 'The Spirit and the Dove', *NTS* 17 (1970-71) 41-67. It is generally read more simply as an adjective: 'like a dove'. See, for example, V. Taylor, *St Mark*, p. 160-161; W. Grundmann, *Markus*, p. 42; R. Pesch, *Markusevangelium*, p. 19.

50 H.C. Waetjen, *Reordering*, pp. 67-74, contrasts the earlier baptism of many 'in the Jordan' and Jesus' baptism 'into the Jordan'. While many did not submit themselves to the full depths of baptism, Jesus did. 'In effect, he drowned; he died eschatologically' (p. 68). Because of this only Jesus is the recipient of the blessings of the new creation. He emerges as 'the New Human Being'.

Jesus has had a visual experience in the gift of the dove. He now *hears* a voice from heaven. The Rabbis often spoke of a voice from above which indicated God's mind (the *bath qôl*), but this is merely a sound, and it is sometimes little more than a shadowy hint. Something more direct is implied here in the clear sound of a voice *(phônê)*. The heavens have been opened, the Spirit has descended, the voice from heaven is nothing less than the voice of God. If the reader has any doubts about this, the author clears them away in his reporting the words from heaven in direct speech: 'You are my Son, the Beloved; with you I am well pleased' (v. 11). Jesus was identified with 'son of God' in v. 1. The reader may wonder if this can be true. Now he is told by the voice of God himself that Jesus is the beloved Son of God.

The words from heaven are close to the words of God reported in Ps 2:7: 'You are my Son' (LXX: *huios mou ei su*). The reader is aware, however, of a change of order in the words, and a greater insistence on the uniqueness of the Son in the Markan use of the Psalm. The direct speech of God places the verb first: 'you are' and is thus able to place a definite article before the title 'son' (*su ei ho huios mou*). This uniqueness is further enhanced by the added adjective, 'the beloved' *(ho agapêtos)*. The reader is aware of the unique relationship between Abraham and Isaac, where the LXX calls Isaac a 'beloved son' (LXX Gen 22:2, 12, 16).[51] 'The heavenly voice identifies Jesus as one having a special relationship with the Father

---

51 See C.R. Kazmierski, *Son of God*, pp. 54-55; R. Pesch, *Markusevangelium*, p. 93. Pesch links this 'only son' theme, via Jewish tradition, to new Adam speculation. I will also suggest that creation motifs lurk behind the final section of the prologue, becoming explicit in v. 13.

— his 'only son'.[52] The final words of God indicate the quality of that relationship: 'with you I am well pleased'.

The reader now has no doubts about *who Jesus is*. The reader has been told that Jesus is the Christ, the son of God, the Lord, the Stronger one, the one who will baptise with the Holy Spirit, the one upon whom the Spirit descends, the *only* Son of God, with whom God is well pleased. But this final qualification raises questions to the reader. There is more to this story than the proclamation of Jesus' dignity. The reader has been well informed on the *facts* about Jesus' relationship with the human story: Christ, messianic son of God, Lord, the Stronger one who will baptise with the Spirit. The reader has also been *told* the facts about the relationship which exists between Jesus as the Son of God in whom his Father is well pleased. These final pieces of information have been provided authoritatively by the voice of God himself. They cannot be doubted, unless one is prepared to doubt the honesty of the relationship between the narrator and the reader.[53]

Before the reader meets the events of Jesus' life, told in the rest of the Gospel narrative, he or she is already aware that this story must be worked out on two levels. On the level of the story of God's people — what one might call the *horizontal* level of the narrative — he is the son of God, the Messiah. This is only possible, however, because of his relationship with God as a Son with whom the Father is well pleased. This may be called

---

52 R.A. Guelich, *Mark*, p. 34.

53 Much modern narrative is told by an unreliable narrator. This is never the case in ancient narratives, and should not be suggested here. The narrator communicates honestly with the reader. On this, see S.D. Moore, *Literary Criticism*, p. 33.

the *vertical* level of the narrative. The two levels coalesce in this final qualification. The Father is well pleased with his Son (vertical) through his messianic action in the human story (horizontal). All of this, however, lies ahead of the reader. *How and why* is God pleased with his only Son? The reader has been given no evidence on *how* Jesus exercises his messianic ministry. He or she will receive a preliminary surprise in the closing statement of the prologue (v. 13), but even greater surprises are in store. The converging of the horizontal and the vertical inevitably produces a cross.

5. Reading Mark vv. 12-13

As yet Jesus' only actions have been to come from Nazareth (v. 9), rise from the water (v. 10) and see the dove (v. 10). These actions have placed Jesus in the right place at the right time, so that things might happen *to* him. The final section of the prologue continues Jesus' passive role: 'The Spirit immediately drove him out into the wilderness' (v. 12).

The Baptist promised that Jesus would baptise with the Spirit (v. 8), the heavens have opened and the Spirit has descended upon him (v. 10). The Spirit has taken possession of Jesus and is the active agent, driving Jesus into the desert. The author uses a strong verb *(ekballei)* to illustrate the imperative of the Spirit's presence in the life of Jesus.[54] Jesus is still the subject of the action of God, driven out into the desert *(eis tên erêmon)*.

---

54 Both Matthew (see Mt 4:1) and Luke (Lk 4:1) tone down the expression, using 'to lead' *(agein)* instead of 'to drive'.

The desert, or the wilderness, appears for the third time in the narrative (see also vv. 3-4). It has a variety of meanings in the Old Testament, Judaism, and in early Christianity but, above all, it is a place of ambiguity. It is a place of refuge, but also of difficult trials; a place of encounter with God, but also of diabolical temptations. The ambivalent character of the symbol of the desert, found in the lives of many Old Testament personalities (for example, Abraham, Elijah and David) has its source in the experience of the Hebrew people after their liberation from Egypt and their crossing of the Reed Sea. The desert was for Israel a place of refuge against aggression, a place of privileged encounter with God, but also a place of difficult physical and moral trials, of temptation and sin.[55] It is against this background that Genesis presents the fallen state of humankind divided against itself, expelled from a garden where creation was in harmony, into a wilderness where the land and all its animal inhabitants rebel against a man and woman who are themselves in conflict (see Gen 2:15-25; 3:14-21).[56]

The reader senses an accumulation of this pre-history to the story of Jesus as v. 13 is read. Taking the number

---

55 On this theme, see E. Corsini, *The Apocalypse. The Perennial Revelation of Jesus Christ* (GNS 5; Wilmington: Michael Glazier, 1983) pp. 216-218; C.E.B. Cranfield, *St Mark*, pp. 41-42. The ambiguous symbol of the desert continues to be used in the early Church, and is particularly well exploited by Athanasius' *Life of Antony*. See R.C. Cregg (ed.) *Athanasius. The Life of Antony and the Letter to Marcellinus* (The Classics of Western Spirituality; London: SPCK, 1980) pp. 33-65. See further P. Brown, *The Body and Society. Men, Women and Sexual Renunciation in Early Christianity* (London: Faber & Faber, 1988) pp. 213-240.

56 It appears to me that the desert in Mark 1:13 is linked with the fall in Genesis, rather than to the Exodus. For the latter, see especially U. Mauser, *Christ in the Wilderness* (SBT 39; London: SCM, 1963) pp. 77-102. For C. Myers, *Binding*, pp. 125-126, it indicates the 'peripheries', as opposed to the priestly/scribal establishment in Jerusalem.

from the forty days and nights during which Moses was
on Mt Sinai without bread nor water (see Ex 34:28; Deut
9:9, 18), repeated in the forty days of Elijah's desert flight
without food (1 Kings 19:4-8), Jesus is in the wilderness
for forty days (v. 13a). He, like Moses and Elijah, experiences the ambiguity of the wilderness. In the midst
of the ambiguity Jesus, like the man and the woman in
Genesis, is tempted by Satan (v. 13b). Adam was tempted
by Satan, fell, and was driven into the wilderness (see
LXX Gen 3:24: 'He [YHWH] drove out *[exebalen]* Adam').
Jesus, filled with the Spirit (v. 10) is driven *(ekballei)* by
that Spirit into the wilderness (v. 12).

Jesus, like Adam, is tempted by Satan, but the narrator
tells of neither fall nor victory. The reader is simply told
that 'he was with the wild beasts; and the angels waited
on to him' (v. 13). For the first time in the narrative Jesus
is actively doing something: he is with the wild beasts.
This may not appear to be important, and is sometimes
taken as a historical note, linking the Gospel to the
experience of Roman martyrdom.[57] But, 'This phrase,
distinctive to Mark's account, holds the key to his temptation narrative'.[58] In the Genesis story Satan's victory
over Adam led to hostility and fear in creation (see Gen
3:14-21; Ps 91:11-13). In the Markan story nothing is
directly reported of Jesus' victory over Satan. Jesus' struggle against evil does not end in the prologue,[59] but he
overcomes the fruits of the first fall: 'he was with the wild

---

57 See, for example, W.L. Lane, *Mark*, p. 15.
58 R.A. Guelich, *Mark*, p. 38.
59 In contrast to Matt 4:11 and Luke 4:13. See W.L. Lane, *Mark*, p. 60-61;
    W. Harrington, *Mark*, p. 8. It is sometimes presupposed that Jesus con-
    quers Satan. See for example, M.J. Lagrange, *Saint Marc*, p. 14; E. Lohmeyer,
    Markus, p. 28.

beasts'. The reader finds that in Jesus from Nazareth the prophetic traditions of Israel have been fulfilled:

> The wolf shall live with the lamb,
> the leopard shall lie down with the kid,
> And the calf and the lion and the fatling together;
> and a little child shall lead them.
> The cow and the bear shall graze,
> their young shall lie down together;
> and the lion shall eat straw like the ox.
> The nursing child shall play over the hole of the asp,
> and the weaned child shall put its hand on the adder's den.
> They will not hurt or destroy
> on all my holy mountain.
> (Is 11:6-9. See also Is 35:3-10; Ezek 34:23-31).

The reader now knows the author's belief that one of the great dreams of first century Judaism has been realised in the coming of Jesus: what was in the beginning has been restored.[60]

This is further reinforced by the indication from the author that Jesus was ministered to by the angels. The reader is familiar with a motif central to the Exodus and to the creation story. The narrator uses the verb 'to minister, to wait upon' *(diakonein)* so that the reader will

---

60 See also H.C. Waetjen, *Reordering*, pp. 74-77. It is beyond the scope of this paper to document the first century Jewish hopes from the restoration of the Adamic situation. See R. Scroggs, *The Last Adam. A Study in Pauline Anthropology* (Oxford: Blackwell, 1966) pp. 1-58; W.D. Davies − D.C. Allison, *A Critical and Exegetical Commentary on the Gospel according to Saint Matthew* (ICC; Edinburgh: T. & T. Clark, 1988) pp. 356-357. In his major study of Mark 1:12-13, E. Best, *The Temptation and the Passion: The Markan Soteriology* (SNTSMS 2; Cambridge: University Press, 1990²) pp. xv-xxiii; 3-60, makes little of creation themes (see pp. xvi-xviii, 6-7). He also claims, however, that Satan is definitely defeated in 1:12-13. He shows this to be the case by arguing the complete absence of a Satan-Jesus conflict through the Gospel. For the opposite case, see J.M. Robinson, *The Problem of History in Mark* (SBT 21; London: SCM Press, 1957) pp. 21-53.

be able to link a number of episodes from the story of Israel with the experience of Jesus, but the notion of feeding and nourishing is close at hand.[61] Repeatedly throughout the desert experience of Israel angels help and guide the wandering people (see Ex 14:19; 23:20, 23; 32:34; 33:2). During Elijah's experience of despair and hunger in the desert, he is served by the angels (see 1 Kings 19:5-7). Although not present in the biblical accounts, Jewish documents refer to the fact that Adam and Eve did not need nourishment in the Garden of Eden. They were fed by the angels (see *Life of Adam and Eve 4; bSanhedrin* 59b).[62]

The reader has been led through a narrative which is dominated by the action of God. Even the brief appearance of the Baptist (vv. 4-8) is part of God's plan, witnessed to by the words of God in vv. 2-3. However, on two occasions before Jesus' appearance in the story, expressions were used which traditionally only applied to YHWH. God spoke of the coming one as 'the Lord' (v. 3) and John the Baptist pointed forward to 'the Mightier one' (v. 7).

Only at the very end of the prologue does Jesus play an active role. He is 'with the wild beasts', served by the angels. His coming has repeated the experience of the original people of God in the desert, and it has restored the original order of God's creation. The promise of 'the

---

61 Unlike Matthew and Luke, where the angels guard Jesus against danger (Mt 4:5-7; Lk 4:8-11). Mt 4:11b repeats Mk 1:13c, but his context gives it a different meaning.
62 On this, see J. Jeremias, Art. *'Adam', TDNT* 1 (1964) 141. See J.H. Charlesworth, *Pseudepigrapha,* Vol. 2, p. 258. For further documentation in support of this suggestion, see W.D. Davies – D.C. Allison, *Saint Matthew,* pp. 356-357.

beginning' in v. 1 (see Gen 1:1) and the coming of the creating Spirit of God in v. 10 (see Gen 1:3) have hinted to the reader that the prologue to the Gospel of Mark may be linked to the prologue to the whole of the human story. But in v. 13 God disappears from the prologue. He has been elided by the narrator, and his place as creator and founder of a people of God has been taken by 'the Lord' (v. 3), 'the Mightier one' (v. 7): Jesus from Nazareth (v. 9).[63]

CONCLUSION

On arrival at v. 13, the reader has been informed that Jesus is the Christ, the Son of God, the Lord, the Stronger one, one who will baptise with the Holy Spirit, who is filled with the Spirit and driven by the Spirit, the unique Son of God in whom the Father is well pleased. The narrator concludes the prologue by eliding God from the action, which he has dominated throughout, and replacing him with Jesus. Jesus from Nazareth takes over God's titles, the Lord (v. 3), the Stronger one (v. 7), and God's action as the giver of the Spirit (v. 8).[64] He restores God's original order in creation (v. 13).

The reader has been told who Jesus is through the prologue. Yet there have been several hints that the Gospel

---

63 Thus, I would claim that v. 13 provides the climax of the prologue, rather than vv. 14-15. See above, note 4.

64 H.C. Waetjen, *Reordering*, p. 22, speaks of Jesus in the prologue as 'God's surrogate'. Here I differ from M.E. Boring's excellent analysis of Mark's prologue ('Mk 1:1-15', pp. 43-81). He rightly sees God as the hidden actor behind the narrative, but claims that 'Mark's introduction subordinates John to Jesus in the mode of narration. This same mode of narration subordinates both John and Jesus to God' (p. 63). Waetjen's idea of 'surrogation' is better than Boring's 'subordination'.

is not simply about who Jesus is. John the Baptist spoke of Jesus' baptising with the Holy Spirit (v. 8), which pointed to a ministry. The word from the opened heavens informed the reader that God was well pleased with his Son (v. 11). God's delight in his Son will flow from the Son's response to the Father. Thus, the reader comes to the end of the prologue informed about *who* Jesus is, but as yet unaware of *how* Jesus is the Christ, the Son of God, the Lord, the Stronger one who baptises with the Holy Spirit; in short, *how* he pleases his Father. J.D. Kingsbury has recently written: 'Since God in Mark's story is the supreme ruler of the universe and all history, the reader recognizes that God's understanding of Jesus' identity is normative'.[65] But *in what way* does Jesus, the Son respond to God's understanding of him; *how* does he restore God's original design and make his Father delight in him? The reader now needs to be shown how this happens in the life-story of Jesus from Nazareth.[66]

The narrative of the Gospel of Mark will often surprise the reader, but it will not disappoint.[67] Jesus opens his ministry by assuming his responsibilities, proclaiming that in *his* coming the Kingdom *of God* is at hand (1:14-15). The new creation is present as the first disciples leave all to walk behind Jesus in obedience to his call

65 J.D. Kinsbury, *Conflict in Mark. Jesus, Authorities, Disciples* (Minneapolis: Fortress Press, 1989) p. 34.

66 It is sometimes claimed that Mark 1:1-13 tells the reader everything that needs to be known. See, for example, M.D. Hooker, *Message*, pp. 5-7. This is not the case, as the reader still has a great deal to learn and experience. On the role of 'telling' and 'showing' in narrative, see W.C. Booth, *Rhetoric*, pp. 3-20; S. Rimmon-Kenan, *Narrative Fiction*, pp. 106-108.

67 See especially M.E. Boring, 'Mark 1:1-15', pp. 63-67. J. Drury, 'Mark', p. 405, puts it well: 'Between the secure understanding given us in its first verse and the radical insecurity and incomprehension of the subsequent tale, Mark's book gets its energy'.

(1:16-20) and as evil is swept aside: demons (1:21-28), sickness and taboo (1:29-31), leprosy and false law (1:39-45). No power of evil seems to stand in the way of the inbreak of God's re-creating presence in Jesus over the first days of the story. However, as in the original creation story, human beings are free to make up their own minds. While the power of demons, sickness, taboo, leprosy and false laws continue to crumble, the people in Jesus' story (who have not read the prologue) begin to complain and to enter into open conflict with him (2:1-3:6).[68]

It will not be long before the reader will find Jesus foretelling that 'the days will come when the bridegroom is taken away from them' (2:20) and the narrator commenting: 'The Pharisees went out, and immediately conspired with the Herodians against him, how to destroy him' (3:6). The way in which the Son delights the Father and thus the way in which Jesus from Nazareth is the Christ may prove to be a surprise to the reader. But, as Wayne Booth has insisted: 'Significant literature arouses suspense not about the "what" but about the "how"'.[69]

---

68 On this, see J. Dewey, *Markan Public Debate. Literary Technique, Concentric Structure, and Theology in Mark 2:1-3:6* (SBLDS 48; Chico: Scholars Press, 1980).
69 W.C. Booth, *Rhetoric*, p. 255.

3 | BEGINNING THE GOSPEL OF MATTHEW
MATTHEW 1:1-2:23

Only the Gospels of Matthew and Luke begin the story of Jesus with narratives about his conception and birth. But the similarity ends there. Our Christmas folk-lore is dominated by the joy of the Lukan story: a virgin mother, angels, Zechariah, Elizabeth, Simeon, Anna and the shepherds. We hear little of a suspected illegitimate birth (Mt 1:18-25) or the wicked, lurking Herod, seeking to slay the child who has to flee for his life (2:13-23). The reader begins the Gospel of Matthew without any knowledge of the Lukan story. The reader will emerge from the Matthean 'beginnings' as the product of a reading experience which depends entirely upon the way in which *this particular story* is told.

WHERE DOES THE BEGINNING END?

Traditionally, the infancy narrative (Mt 1-2) is seen as the introduction to the Gospel of Matthew. The body of the Gospel is dominated by the five discourses unique to the First Gospel (Mt 5-7; 10:1-11:1; 13:2-53; 18:1-35; 24-25). Each discourse is prefaced by narratives from the ministry of Jesus (Mt 3:1-4:25; 8:1-9:38; 11:2-12:50; 13:54-17:27; 19:1-23:29). Matching the infancy narrative, and serving as a conclusion to the Gospel, is the story of Jesus' passion and resurrection (Mt 26-28).[1]

This position has been challenged in recent years, as many suggest that the introduction to the Gospel runs beyond the infancy narrative into the report on the Baptist's preaching and activity, including the baptism of Jesus.[2] It appears to me that more recent critics are correct in suggesting that the Gospel's 'prologue' runs into the days of the Baptist. However, where does the beginning end? There are weighty reasons for choosing 4:11 as the end of the beginning and 4:12 as the start of Jesus' ministry. It is here that Matthew, in his own way, joins Mark in having Jesus appear in Galilee (vv. 12-16) proclaiming: 'Repent, for the kingdom of heaven is at hand' (v. 17).[3]

---

1 The great champion of this approach was B.W. Bacon, *Studies in Matthew* (London: Constable, 1930) and Ibid., 'The "Five Books" of Matthew against the Jews', *The Expositor* 15 (1918) 55-66. It is still followed in a very good recent commentary: J.P. Meier, *Matthew* (NTM 3; Wilmington: Michael Glazier, 1980).

2 See especially J.D. Kingsbury, *Matthew: Structure, Christology, Kingdom* (Philadelphia: Fortress Press, 1975) pp. 1-39. For a survey, see D. Senior, *What are they saying about Matthew?* (New York: Paulist Press, 1983) pp. 20-27.

3 For this decision, see U. Luz, *Matthew 1-7. A Commentary* (Edinburgh: T. & T. Clark, 1990) pp. 192-194; F.J. Matera, 'The Plot of Matthew's Gospel', *CBQ* 49 (1987) 246-247. As well as the link with the Galilean setting in both Mark 1:14-15 and Matthew 4:12-17, there is a series of temporal links across 3:1-4:11 which separates it from 4:12: 'In those days' (3:1: *en tais hēmerais*); 'seeing' (3:7: *idōn*); 'then' (3:13: *tote*); 'then' (4:1: *tote*); 'then' (4:11: *tote*). This is broken in 4:12 by the use of the aorist participle 'having heard' *(akousas)* and the aorist passive 'had been arrested' *(paredothē)*.

Although the literary 'beginning' of Matthew's Gospel may be 1:1-4:11, I will limit this study to the infancy narrative (Mt 1-2). My decision is necessitated by a need to comment on a restricted amount of material, but there are also good literary reasons for studying Matthew 1-2 on its own right. The difference in literary form and the undivided attention this section gives to the perfection of God's plan in the fulfilment of God's word indicate that it stands on its own as the beginning of the beginnings of the story of Jesus.

Unlike Luke 1-2, Matthew has separated the person of John the Baptist from the infancy. The Baptist will not appear until the latter part of the introduction (see 3:1-17), introducing Jesus as the 'coming one' (see 3:11-12) and the 'beloved Son' (see 3:13-17), claims which will be tested by the devil in the wilderness (see 4:1-11).[4] Such claims and their vindication are essential to the theological preparation of the reader who begins to read the story of Jesus' life and ministry in 4:12. Nevertheless, they are not entirely new to the reader who comes to 3:1 armed with the information provided by the infancy narrative. Thus, while not denying the importance of 3:1-4:11 as part of the beginning of Matthew's story, I will limit myself to following the reader through Matthew 1-2.[5]

B.B. Scott, 'The Birth of the Reader', *Sem* 52 (1990) p. 98, note 4, suggests that 4:12-25 is 'a transition': 'The hearer of the story needs narrative time to shift from one unit to another'.

4   These elements (in a briefer form) were found in Mark's prologue (Mk 1:1-13). They remain part of the literary and theological prologue to the Gospel of Matthew.

5   Rightly J.P. Meier, *Matthew*, p. 1, claims that Matthew 1-2 is 'weaving together in miniature a number of significant themes which will be played out at length as the gospel progresses'.

THE SHAPE OF THE NARRATIVE

The author of this Gospel has been called 'meticulous
Matthew',[6] and the term is well-earned. After an intro-
ductory proclamation (1:1), the reader meets a long
genealogy (1:2-17), a description of how the birth of
Jesus took place (1:18-23), the coming of the wise men
to Bethlehem, via Jerusalem and an encounter with
Herod (2:1-12), and a series of events which flow from
Herod's concern over the newly-born King: the flight
into Egypt (2:13-15), the slaying of the male infants
in Bethlehem (2:16-18), and the return from Egypt
(2:19-23).

It is sometimes said that the first chapter of Matthew's
Gospel – the genealogy and the birth of Jesus – and
the second – the visit of the wise men and the subsequent flight and persecution – are independent. Whatever
may have been Matthew's sources for his tales, he wanted
them to be read as one.[7] The clearest sign of this is his
rhythmic concluding of episodes across all the infancy
stories with indications that each episode fulfils the Scriptures (see 1:22-23; 2:5-6, 15, 17-18, 23). After decades of
debate, it is now widely accepted that Matthew did not
compose a narrative to comment upon the Old Testament
citations, but he added the Old Testament passages to his

---

6   P.F. Ellis, *Matthew: His Mind and His Message* (Collegeville: Liturgical Press,
    1974) pp. 27-98, uses this title for his chapter on the literary structure of
    the Gospel.
7   On Matthew's sources, see R.E. Brown, *The Birth of the Messiah* (Garden
    City: Doubleday, 1977) pp. 96-121; W.D. Davies – D.C. Allison, *The Gospel
    According to Saint Matthew* (ICC; Edinburgh: T. & T. Clark, 1988)
    pp. 190-195. On the thematic unity of Matthew 1-2, see the rich study of
    D. Patte, *The Gospel According to Matthew. A Structural Commentary on
    Matthew's Faith* (Philadelphia: Fortress, 1987) pp. 16-42.

already existing narratives.[8] They are a particularly effective Matthean contribution to the overall shape and unity of the infancy story. But they are, above all, an important indication of the author's point of view: the coming of Jesus is the fulfilment of God's plan.

It has been suggested that the author constructed the present narrative to begin the Gospel by immediately providing answers to two questions: 'Who is Jesus?', and 'Where did he come from?'[9] There is much to be said for such a claim, but the focus of this approach is too Christological. The initial proclamation of Jesus as Son of David and Son of Abraham (1:1), the genealogy (1:2-17) and the birth of Jesus as the Emmanuel (1:23) point to who Jesus is, but these claims are told in a way which shows the fulfilment of God's sacred history and the fulfilment of God's word. The concentration upon Jerusalem (2:1), Bethlehem (2:5-6, 8, 16), Egypt (2:13-15) Ramah (2:18) and Nazareth (2:23) focuses upon Jesus' place of origin, but all locations are explicitly mentioned as the fulfilment of the Scriptures. The interest is not geographical, but theological, in the strict sense. I will continue to use the categories of 'who' and 'where from', as I also

8 For a comprehensive study, see G.M. Soares Prabhu, *The Formula Quotations in the Infancy Narratives of Matthew* (AnBib 63; Rome: Biblical Institute Press, 1976). See also R.E. Brown, *Birth*, pp. 96-104.3; E. Schweizer, *The Good News according to Matthew* (London: SPCK, 1975) pp. 27-28. But see F. Kermode, 'Matthew', in *The Literary Guide*, p. 394: 'best thought of as free narrative compositions based on selected Old Testament *données*'.

9 On this, see the seminal work of K. Stendahl, '*Quis et Unde?* An Analysis of Matthew 1-2', in G. Stanton, (ed.), *The Interpretation of Matthew* (IRT 3; London: SPCK, 1983) pp. 56-66. (Originally published in 1960). See the further development of this scheme into 'who – how – where – whence' in R.E. Brown, *Birth*, pp. 50-54. For my own earlier study along these lines, see F.J. Moloney, 'The infancy narrative in Matthew', in H. McGinlay (ed.), *The Year of Matthew* (Melbourne: Desbooks/JBCE, 1983) 1-9.

believe that they determine the shape of the narrative, but more attention needs to be given to the dominant role of God. God cannot be strictly called a character in the narrative, as he never appears in person, but he is an all-pervasive presence. The child never speaks, is spoken to or acts. He is described, born, worshipped and taken to Egypt and Nazareth. He is totally receptive, and never active in the story.[10] But God, through his agents, the angel of God and the prophets, is omnipresent.[11] As with the prologue to the Gospel of Mark, the question 'who is Jesus?' is important to the narrative, but he is who he is only because he is the fulfilment of God's action in both the pre-history and the events of the narrative itself. Precisely because of God's plan, the question of 'who is Jesus?' does not cease at 1:25, as the narrator moves on to tell of Jesus' origins in 2:1-23. It is all-pervading.[12]

I would thus suggest the following shape for the beginnings of Matthew's Gospel:

A — 1:1-25: The Person of Jesus: the Fulfilment of God's Design.

(a) The initial proclamation states boldly that Jesus is Son of David and Son of Abraham (1:1), but this claim

---

10 M.H. Abrams, *A Glossary of Literary Terms* (New York: Holt, Rinehart and Winston, 1988⁵) p. 22, defines 'characters' as 'the persons presented in a dramatic or narrative work, who are interpreted by the reader as being endowed with moral, dispositional and emotional qualities that are expressed in what they say — the dialogue — and by what they do — the action'. In these terms, Jesus certainly does not qualify as a character in Matthew 1-2, while God, who 'dialogues' a great deal, might. See also S. Chatman, *Story and Discourse*, pp. 106-145; M.A. Powell, *What is Narrative Criticism?*, pp. 51-58.

11 The angel of God only reports what the one who sent him wishes to say. On this, see H. Bietenhard, Art. 'Angel, Messenger, Gabriel, Michael', in C. Brown (ed.), *The New International Dictionary of New Testament Theology* (Exeter: Paternoster Press, 1975) pp. 101-103. See esp. p. 101.

12 Indeed, as U. Luz, *Matthew*, p. 102, note 2, points out, both of these questions (provenance and Messiah) continue into chapter 4.

is proved by means of a God-directed genealogy: the Son of Abraham, Son of David is Jesus, who is called Christ (1:2-17).

(b) The story of the annunciation to Joseph and his unquestioning response to God assures Jesus' Davidic line, as Joseph is the Davidide, but it also claims that he is Saviour, of the Holy Spirit and Emmanuel – God with us (1:18-25).

B — 2:1-23: The Person and the Origins of Jesus: the Fulfilment of God's Design.

(a) The wise men, led by a heavenly sign to Jerusalem, introduces a new theme: Jesus is 'King of the Jews'. His birth in Bethlehem fulfils God's prophecy and reinforces the narrator's earlier insistence that he is 'the Christ'. The wise men bring gifts to a royal figure, fulfilling further promises of the word of God through his prophet (2:1-12).

(b) The flight to Egypt and the slaying of the innocents establish that Jesus is repeating in his story the story of Moses. Another feature is added to Jesus: he is the new and perfect Moses-figure. The Scriptures are fulfilled when Jesus comes out of Egypt (Hos 11:1) and, as at the birth of Moses (see Ex 1:15-22), innocent Hebrew children are slain at the birth of Jesus (Mt 2:13-18).

(c) Only at the end of the narrative does the question of Jesus *of Nazareth* emerge as a major theme. Everything the reader has encountered so far would indicate that he should be called Jesus *of Bethlehem*, but he was not known as such. The infancy narrative concludes by showing the reader how Jesus came to be called a Nazarene (2:19-23). Even this claim, however, is not simply directed to Jesus' place of origin (where from?), but above all to the quality of his response to God (who?), in fulfilment of all that had been promised by God's prophets.

As with the prologue to the Gospel of Mark, the reader will come to the reading experience of the life and ministry of Jesus with some firm ideas about who Jesus is. The reader is also aware that none of this would be possible without the action of God. Although, quite properly, God can never appear in person, the angel of God and the words of the prophets ensure that the reader understands the events of the infancy narrative as the result of God's plan and God's initiative. The claims of the prologue will be tested by the way Jesus lives, forms disciples and makes demands upon all who would follow him, dies and sends out his newly-formed community to the ends of the earth. But the affirmation of the risen Lord at the end of the story, 'I am with you always' (28:20), is only possible because of the promise of the word of God at the beginning of the story: 'His name will be called Emmanuel (which means God with us)' (1:23).[13]

READING THE NARRATIVE

1. Reading Matthew 1:1

The reader recognises two possible meanings for the first words of the story: 'The book of the genealogy' *(biblos*

---

13 On the relationship between the beginning and the end of a narrative, see
    M.C. Parsons, 'Reading a Beginning', pp. 13-18. In the conclusion of Mat-
    thew's Gospel (28:16-20) Jesus takes on roles traditionally attributed only
    to God. On this, see F.J. Moloney, *The Living Voice*, pp. 118-123.

geneseôs). Is the reader beginning a book which is purely a genealogy, or a book which in some way will repeat the creative action of God? Already in the Old Testament the author's opening phrase has been used to introduce a description of the original creation (LXX Gen 2:4. MT: *sêper tôledôt.* See also 5:1). The reader does not know, but reads on with both possibilities in mind.[14] This book is about a person called Jesus who is the Christ, the Son of David and the Son of Abraham (1:1).[15]

The reader, credited with a knowledge of Jewish messianic expectations, would have no difficulties in accepting the possibility that the person called Jesus was the Christ, and that he was such as a royal messianic son of David.[16] But 'son of Abraham' introduces a notion which is broader than the usual Jewish messianic hope. Although it was used to speak of someone who was of authentic Jewish blood (see, for example, Jn 8:33; Heb 2:16-17), Abraham himself was a Gentile by birth, and as YHWH called him away from his country, his kindred and his father's house, he had been promised: 'I will make of you a great nation, and I will bless you and make your name great, so that you will be a blessing ... By you all the families of the earth shall bless themselves' (Gen 12:3). Later he is again promised: 'Behold my covenant is with you and you shall be the father of many nations' (Gen 17:4. See also 15:5).

---

14 See W.D. Davies – D.C. Allison, *Saint Matthew*, pp. 149-155.
15 Although he was 'Jesus of Nazareth', the compound 'Jesus Christ' quickly became a proper name (see Rom 1:1; Gal 1:1; Jas 1:1; Rev 22:21). Due to the appearance of 'the Christ' in 1:17 and its being in apposition with 'son of David' in 1:1, it appears that the expression 'Christ' has a messianic content in 1:1 (see also 2:4; 16:16, 20; 22:42; 24:5, 23; 26:63, 68). See J.D. Kingsbury, *Structure*, pp. 96-97. Against U. Luz, *Matthew*, p. 104.
16 See J.D. Kingsbury, *Structure*, pp. 99-103.

In the new creation which will take place in Jesus the highest of Jewish messianic hopes are achieved in this Son of David. But God's promises to unite and bless all nations will also be realised in this Son of Abraham.[17] The reader has already met one of the objectives of the Gospel of Matthew: God wishes to unite both Jew and Gentile into one community through Jesus Christ.

2. Reading Matthew 1:2-17

As the reader works his way through the long list of fathers, occasionally interrupted by the name of a mother, he or she becomes aware that a carefully constructed list is being read. He or she reads of 14 generations from Abraham to David (a period of roughly 1000 years), then another 14 generations from David to the Babylonian exile (about 400 years) and a final 14 generations from the Exile to Jesus the Christ (about 600 years). God has directed a history of salvation from Abraham to Jesus Christ. The list of names already makes this point, but the narrator's comment in v. 17 informs the reader further of God's direction of the generations from Abraham to the Christ.[18]

The claims of 1:1 have now been proved by a genealogy which shows that God has designed the history of his people. Jesus is the Christ, a direct product of the line

---

17 Against R.H. Gundry, *Matthew. A Commentary on His Literary and Theological Art* (Grand Rapids: Eerdmans, 1982) p. 13. He suggests that David is the son of Abraham in v. 1, and not Jesus.

18 The use of 3 x 14 generations to convey this idea has given rise to many speculations. For a survey, see R.E. Brown, *Birth*, pp. 74-81. Most likely the use of 3 rests on the traditional understanding (in many cultures) of 3 as a perfect number, and 14 is made up of the Hebrew letters/numbers *d-w-d* which indicate 'David' and have the numerical value of 14. The perfection of the Davidic line is indicated.

of David, in fulfilment of Jewish messianic hopes. Without actually citing the Scriptures, the genealogy has already shown that Jesus fulfils the hopes of Israel. But the genealogy goes beyond David to Abraham. Jesus is also the son of Abraham. He fulfills the promises of God to 'all the families of the earth' (see Gen 12:3). Not only the hopes of Israel are fulfilled; in fulfilment of God's word, all the nations of the earth shall be blessed in him.

There have also been five women in Jesus' line: Tamar (v. 3; see Gen 46:12), Rahab (v. 5a; see Josh 2:1-21; 6:17-25), Ruth (v. 5b; see Ruth 4:18-22), Bathsheba (v. 6; see 2 Sam 11:2-26; 1 Kings 1:11-40) and Mary, 'of whom Jesus was born, who is called Christ' (v. 16). A line of women, crucial to the ongoing story of God's people, have courageously accepted the strangeness of God's ways to eventually produce the Son of David, Son of Abraham.[19] Each one of these women has, in some way, had the courage to risk standing outside accepted *mores* to continue God's line. Not only has the reader met a clear statement of who Jesus is, but, for the first time, a hint of the radical nature of the response required from those who will accept God's designs as they are revealed in Jesus the Christ, the Son of David, the son of Abraham has been encountered.

3. Reading Matthew 1:18-25

Already in the genealogy the reader has been made aware that, even though it is Joseph who belongs to the line of David, Jesus is not his physical son. The steady rhythm

---

19 For a discussion of the women in Matthew 1:2-17, see F.J. Moloney, *Woman: First Among the Faithful. A New Testament Study* (Melbourne: Collins Dove, 1984) pp. 33-37. See also B.B. Scott, 'The Birth', pp. 85-88.

of father begetting son is broken as the genealogy comes to a close: 'And Jacob the Father of Joseph the husband of Mary, of whom Jesus was born, who is called Christ' (v. 16). How did Jesus become a Son of David, if he was not the son of a Davidide? The narrator immediately indicates that this issue is now to be faced: 'Now the birth of Jesus Christ took place *in this way*' (v. 18). The omniscient narrator informs the reader that Mary, before she and Joseph came together, was with child by the Holy Spirit (v. 18). The first person to enter the action of the story is God, filling Mary with a child through the Holy Spirit. Joseph knows nothing of this. The reader 'knows that Mary is both potentially publicly shamed and yet divinely honored'.[20] However, Joseph is a 'just man' *(dikaios)*, a man who lives according to the law of God. God comes first in his life. He and Mary are already betrothed and he is thus in a position where he can use a more lenient method of divorce, rather than publicly declare her an adulteress (v. 19).[21]

In the midst of his holy confusion, an angel of the Lord appears in a dream to Joseph with a command which informs Joseph of the role of the Holy Spirit in the conception of the child at the moment being carried by his wife (v. 20).[22] Joseph now knows what the reader knows.

---

20 B.B. Scott, 'The Birth', p. 89.
21 For a discussion of the interpretation of *dikaios*, see R.E. Brown, *Birth*, pp. 125-128. On the divorce question, see R.H. Gundry, *Matthew*, pp. 21-22. However, I disagree with Gundry's suggestion that Joseph acts 'in deference to the Holy Spirit'. He does not know of the Holy Spirit at this stage of the narrative. Only the author and the reader do. See B.B. Scott, 'The Birth', pp. 89-90.
22 E. Schweizer, *Matthew*, p. 29, claims that 'Joseph is portrayed in terms similar to those used in contemporary Jewish circles to depict the father of Moses'. He cites Josephus, *Antiquities* ii. 212, 16 and Pseudophilo *Antiquities* ix. 10. Both speak of dream appearances.

He knows that God has entered in a surprising and dramatic way into his personal life. How will he react? The reader is left wondering about Joseph as titles of honour are heaped upon a child who has not even seen the light of day. Not only is he 'of the Holy Spirit', but his name is to be Jesus 'for he will save his people from their sins' (v. 21).[23] The presence of a child conceived by the Holy Spirit who will save his people from their sins fulfils the promise of Isaiah 7:14: 'A virgin shall conceive and bear a son and his name shall be called Emmanuel' (vv. 22-23). The author's interest is not in the virgin-mother,[24] but in the fulfilment of the prophetic promise that a child about to be born will prove to be God with his people. Jesus' being the fulfilment of the God's prophetic word, implicit in the genealogy, has now become explicit. God's angel and God's word explain to both Joseph and the reader the origin and the destiny of the son of Mary.

Although showing little interest in the virgin-mother, the author affirms the virginal conception of Jesus with a clarity not paralleled by Luke.[25] Jesus is certainly the fulfilment of all that God has promised his people, and in this sense he continues and fulfils the history of God's people. But his virginal conception indicates that something new is happening. God is entering history in an unprecedented way. A virginal conception is not just another event in human history. The coming of the

---

23 For the importance of the name 'Jesus' in Matthew's Gospel, see J.D. Kingsbury, *Matthew as Story* (Philadelphia: Fortress Press, 1988²) pp. 45-47.

24 Matthew's use of the passage in his context is only possible because of the LXX translation of Isaiah 7:14, where the Hebrew word *'almâh* (girl of child-bearing age) is translated *parthenos* (virgin). For detailed discussions of this issue, see R.E. Brown, *Birth*, pp. 143-153; W.D. Davies – D.C. Allison, *Saint Matthew*, pp. 214-217.

25 Luke does affirm Jesus' virginal conception, but in a more nuanced fashion.

Emmanuel not only fulfils the prophecy of Isaiah, it announces that in a new way, God is with his people.[26] Although never present, God is the only active character (through his agents) in all that has been reported so far.

Only now can the narrator return to Joseph. The reader finds that the passage comes to a satisfactory conclusion as Joseph does exactly as the angel had commanded him.[27] The direct speech of the angel becomes the reported speech of the narrator: Joseph took Mary to his home as wife, he did not have intercourse with her, and he called the child Jesus.[28] If the radical obedience of the women in the genealogy had facilitated God's saving history, their openness to God's ways is matched by the response of Joseph. In taking Mary as wife to his own home he has had to accept the strangeness of God's ways in accepting as his own a child who could well be regarded as illegitimate. In this way Jesus became the Son of David. Joseph's response is presented to the reader as an essential part of God's design.[29]

The reader continues to learn about Jesus, the fulfilment of God's promises: Christ, Son of David, son of

---

26 See, on this 'continuity/discontinuity', J.P. Meier, *Matthew*, pp. 6-7. See also E. Schweizer, *Matthew*, pp. 32-35.

27 According to R. Pesch, 'Eine Alttestamentliche Ausführungsformel im Matthäusevangelium. Redaktionsgeschichtliche und exegetische Beobachtungen', *BZ* 10 (1966) 220-245; 11 (1967) 79-85, vv. 24-25 represent an obedience formula used in the Old Testament to express human submission to the will of God.

28 The expression 'knew her not *until (heôs)* she had borne a son' says nothing about what happened *after* she had borne the son. It neither destroys nor defends the traditional doctrine of the perpetual virginity of Mary. On this, see R.E. Brown, *Birth*, p. 132. See J.P. Meier, *Matthew*, p. 9: 'The main concern for Mt at the end of the story is not the virginity of Mary but the function of Joseph, who places Jesus in the Davidic line by adoption'.

29 See B.B. Scott, 'The Birth', pp. 90-91. Scott shows that Joseph, as well as Mary, 'to maintain his true righteousness ... must suffer public shame'.

Abraham, of the Holy Spirit and Emmanuel. The reader also learns about the demands which God makes upon those whom he calls to play a part in his designs. It will often touch them at the most intimate level of their being. The stories of the five women and Joseph inform the reader of that.[30]

4. Reading Matthew 2:1-12

The narrative link between 1:24-25 and 2:1 is not as loose as is sometimes suggested.[31] The reader learns that a child is born and accepted by Joseph (1:24-25), and then goes on to learn the time and the place of that birth: in Bethlehem in the days of Herod, the King. Joseph is not only of the line of David (see 1:16), but he also lives in the city of David (2:1).

The wise men from the east come to Jerusalem raising a serious problem by saying: 'Where is he who has been born King of the Jews?' The narrator has already told the reader that Herod was the King. Now there are two kings in the story. Conflict is inevitable. The wise men seek a King because they have seen a 'star at its rising'.[32] Their experience reflects the widespread idea that each person has his or her star, the important and rich people a bright one, and others an insignificant one which appears at birth and is extinguished at death.[33]. The reader is

30 This has been well presented by B.B. Scott, 'The Birth', pp. 84-93, in his explanation of 1:1-25. The theme also runs into 2:1-23.
31 Rightly F.W. Beare, *The Gospel According to Matthew. A Commentary* (Oxford: Blackwell, 1981) pp. 75-76.
32 As in the NRSV, rather than 'his star in the East' (RSV). On this understanding of *ton astera en têi anatolêi*, see U. Luz, *Matthew*, p. 128, note 1.
33 See U. Luz, *Matthew*, p. 135. For classical and Jewish background for this idea, see p. 135, note 43 and R.E. Brown, *Birth*, pp. 170-171. One of the

aware that a bright star which led wise men from the East to Jerusalem must mark the birth of an important figure. Something outside human control is in the story. The use of the aorist passive participle, translated in the NRSV as 'who has been born' *(techtheis)* affirms this awareness. The divine passive indicates God's action. Heavenly signs lead foreigners on a search for something that God is doing. Such an impression is further strengthened by the confession of the wise men that they have come to worship, to bow down to the ground in obeissance *(proskunein)* to the new-born King.[34]

It is not surprising that Herod, the King, was troubled. The wise men are reporting a direct threat to his authority. What is surprising is that 'all of Jerusalem' is also troubled. The verb used to speak of the consternation of Herod the King and all of Jerusalem with him *(tarassein)* refers to a deep emotional shock. This experience leads to a gathering of 'all the chief priests and scribes of the people'. There is a widespread negative reaction to the question of the wise men. The reader senses the introduction of an ominous note. Indeed, although the reader is not yet aware of it, the author has the passion of Jesus in mind. At Jesus' trial and crucifixion the secular ruler in Jerusalem and 'all the chief priests and scribes of the people' (27:1) will line up against Jesus. In the passion 'all the people' (27:25) will accept the responsibility for Jesus' blood. That is yet to come for the reader, but on reading

characters in Rogers and Hammerstein's modern musical, *Paint your Wagon*, still sings, 'I was born under a wandering star'.

34 The reader meets the verb *proskunein* for the first time. It will be regularly used throughout the narrative to indicate a correct response to Jesus (see 2:11; 8:2; 9:18; 14:33; 15:25; 18:26; 20:20; 28:9, 17). See H. Greeven, Art. *'proskuneô, proskunêtês'*, in *TDNT* VI (1968) 758-766. See esp. pp. 763-764.

the passion story the reader will recall that from birth Jesus was destined to be a suffering Messiah and King.

The wise men's question concerning the child-king's place of birth receives the correct answer. Through a combination of several Old Testament texts (predominantly Mic 5:1, but also 2 Sam 5:2 and 1 Chron 11:2), the wise men are directed to Bethlehem, and they are told that the child will be a ruler who will govern Israel (vv. 5-6). Despite their perturbed state, Jewish authorities give the correct answer. There can be no resisting the fulfilment of the prophetic promise. God's word will stand forever (see Is 40:8). The reader knows the response to the wise men is correct, and is also aware that the narrative is proceeding along God's lines, but the reader also suspects that the people who give the response may not be prepared to accept their new-born King.

Another major theme has been introduced. The wise men come to the place, to the people and to the book where God's saving history can be discovered: Jerusalem, all the people and their religious leaders, the words written by the prophet. Israel knows that the answer to its hope can only be found in the fulfilment of God's promises to them. Israel is the place where God's sacred history has been enacted. The wise men must go to Jerusalem if they hope to find the solution to the mystery of the King of the Jews, the Messiah. However, traditional Israel will reject Jesus as Messiah and King and in doing so will reject God's plan. Who then, is the true people of God? God's saving action is shifting away from its traditional locus towards a new chosen people, and the first people to seek its King are Gentiles.

The reader's suspicions about possible hostility towards the new-born King are immediately confirmed. Herod summons the wise men 'secretly'. Stealth has entered the story. He wants to know when the star appeared (v. 7). This will prove important for a later event, but Herod's duplicity is heightened in his request that the wise men find the child so that they might bring him word, 'that I too may come and worship *(proskunein)* him' (v. 8). The reader knows that the wise men came to worship the new-born King in response to a heavenly sign and a belief that God's action was somehow involved in the birth of a King (see v. 2). Herod's motives already seem more directed towards the preservation of his own plans than any acceptance of the plan of God.

Having learnt from Jerusalem and its prophetic tradi-tion that the child will be born in Bethlehem, the wise men travel towards that city, guided by the star which comes to rest over the place where the child was. The star has now changed its character. The wise men had earlier spoken of the rising of a star which marked the birth of a King. Now the star is moving, leading the rejoicing searchers towards the child (vv. 9-10). Their jour-ney brings them to mother and child. They fall down and worship, opening their gifts of gold, frankincense and myrrh. The reader once again senses the fulfilment of God's prophetic word:

> May the kings of Tarshish and of the isles render
> him tribute,
> May the kings of Sheba and Seba bring gifts!
> May all kings fall down before him,
> all nations serve him (Ps. 72:10-11).
> All those from Sheba shall come.
> They shall bring gold and frankincense,
> and shall proclaim the praise of the Lord (Is 60:6).

Foreigners have come, bringing gifts in homage to the King, God's royal son (see Ps 72:1).

But what of the star? The reader, well versed in the traditions of Israel, recalls an earlier time in Israel's sacred history when a star announced the coming of a messianic King. In Num 24 the foreign visionary Balaam had been asked to condemn Israel. But he was unable to resist the inspiration of YHWH. He proclaimed an oracle about a future ruler (24:17). In both the Hebrew (MT) and the LXX Balaam speaks of a star which will come forth (MT) or arise (LXX) from Jacob, a sceptre (MT) or a man (LXX) from Israel. The Aramaic Targums take this interpretation even further into a directly messianic interpretation of the star:

> 'I see him but not now; I behold him but not nigh.
> When a king shall arise out of Jacob,
> and the Messiah be anointed from Israel,
> he will slay the princes of Moab and reign over
> all the children of men'.[35]

The Targums reflect the popular understanding of the biblical text, and this is the background to the star which settles over Jesus. The wise men have no hesitation in accepting that they have found the messianic King, and they fall to their knees in adoration, bringing their gifts. The opening proclamation and the genealogy (1:1-17) both asserted (v. 1) and offered physical proof (vv. 2-16) that Jesus was the son of Abraham, in whom all nations would be blessed. The wise men from the East show such blessing

---

35 The Targums reflect the text of the Bible as it was read and interpreted in Aramaic-speaking Synagogue worship. In general, see M. McNamara, *Targum and Testament. Aramaic Paraphrases of the Hebrew Bible: A Light on the New Testament* (Shannon: Irish University Press, 1972). For the English text of the Targum given here, which I have somewhat modernised, see J.W. Etheridge, *The Targums of Onkelos and Jonathan Ben Uzziel on the Pentateuch with the Fragments of the Jerusalem Targum from the Chaldee* (New York: KTAV, 1968) pp. 309-311.

taking place already in the presence of the newly born King.

The narrator then adds a final remark concerning the wise men. Like Joseph, who responded without hesitation to the command of God which came in a dream, they return home without contacting Herod. The wise men embody two essential elements of the narrative: their *coming* to the new-born King fulfils God's prophetic promise as Gentiles come towards Jesus, the Son of Abraham, and their *departure* indicates how one must respond to God. They accept the command of the angel of the Lord without question.

The birth of Jesus in the Davidic city of Bethlehem instructs the reader on Jesus' messianic status, but the focus of the narrative is not upon the city of Bethlehem.[36] Jesus' being the the King of the Jews (v. 2, 6, 11), the Messiah (v. 4, 9-10) and the Son of David still forms the background to the story of the wise men. However, most of all he is now clearly presented as the son of Abraham. Furthermore, the reader has had the first hints that the future of the royal messianic Son of God will be marked by opposition and violence from the people who had been God's chosen people: Israel. The inability of God's original chosen people to accept the new-born King has been matched by Gentiles who come to offer him homage and obedience. Not only is the sub-theme of the origins of Jesus present in the passage's concentration upon Bethlehem, but there are clouds gathering which point towards his destiny: death and resurrection which will

---

36 It is here that both Stendhal's insistence on the 'where' and Brown's modification of the scheme to 'where from and where to' underplay the important continuation of the central theme: Jesus as the fulfilment of the promises of God. See above, note 9.

lead to the final commission that the disciples must baptise all nations (see 28:19). It is not enough to stress Jesus' fulfilment of God's messianic promises to Israel. There is a darker side to God's plan which must also be fulfilled. These themes become more central in the final section of the narrative.

5. Reading Matthew 2:13-23

The final section of the narrative dedicated to Jesus' birth and infancy is made up of three brief scenes during which the narrator addresses the reader at all times (vv. 13-15; vv. 16-18; vv. 19-23).[37] There are only two forms of interruption to the rapid reporting of the narrator. On one occasion an 'angel of the Lord' will speak to Joseph (v. 13) and on three occasions the narrator, claiming that the events he has reported fulfil the promises of scripture, will cite 'the prophets' (vv. 15, 18, 23). Thus, through this section only the voices of the narrator and of God are heard.[38] The narration is dominated by evil designs of others upon Jesus, while the voice of God shows that these designs are nevertheless part of God's saving plans for Jesus − and for the reader.

Having dismissed the wise men, the narrator returns to Joseph, who again experiences the direct intervention of God, through the command of the angel of God. The command to fly to Egypt is motivated by the plan of Herod 'to search for the child, to destroy him' (v. 13). The suspicions of the reader, first aroused by Herod's summoning

---

37 On the increasing speed of the narrative, see R.A. Edwards, *Matthew's Story of Jesus* (Philadelphia: Fortress Press, 1985) pp. 14-15.
38 The angel of God speaks the word of God. See above, note 11.

of the wise men and speaking to them 'secretly' (2:7),
are now confirmed. The reader is now fully aware that
Herod's desire to 'worship' *(proskunein)* the new-born King
was hypocrisy (see 2:8). There are no half-way measures
in Herod's plans. He seeks to 'destroy' *(apoluein)* Jesus.
The same verb will return in 27:20: 'Now the chief priests
and the elders persuaded the people to ask for Barabbas
and destroy Jesus'.[39]

Continuing the earlier response to the word of God
(1:24-25), a response which has been repeated by the wise
men (v. 12), the narrator reports Joseph's obedience by having him do exactly what the words of the angel commanded. The only addition to the words of the angel,
'by night' adds to the radical nature of the obedience.
The reader presupposes that Joseph dreams by night, and
thus the departure is immediate. The reader is then taken
further into the narrative through a prolepsis: the family
remained in Egypt 'until the death of Herod' (v. 15a). The
next section (vv. 16-18) returns to the time of the story:
Herod is still very much alive. But the reader is already
secure in the knowledge that Jesus is not part of the slaying. Herod will die before Jesus!

God enters the story once more as the narrator tells
the reader that this was to fulfil what the Lord had spoken
by the prophet, 'Out of Egypt have I called my son' (v. 13).
The quotation of Hosea 11:1 continues the author's focus
upon Jesus as the fulfilment of God's promises. For the
first time in the narrative, the reader has been told explicitly that Jesus is God's Son. This claim for Jesus is,
without doubt, the major thrust of the passage. However,

39 See W.D. Davies – D.C. Allison, *Saint Matthew*, p. 260.

there is more to it. The orginal prophecy recalled the Exodus, as Moses led the people of God away from Egypt into the promised land. There is now the suggestion that Jesus may be the new and perfect Moses.[40]

Joseph, his wife and her child are left out of the story for the moment as the narrator reports Herod's rage. It leads to the slaying of all the male children under two years of age, and the reader again looks back to Herod's earlier secret interview with the wise men, when he 'ascertained from them what time the star had appeared' (2:7). Importantly, the reason given by the narrator for Herod's rage is no longer his fear of the threat of a royal child, but because he saw that he had been 'mocked' by the wise men (v. 16a). The verb used here *(empaizein)* is found in four other places in Matthew's Gospel. On one occasion Jesus foretells that he will be delivered to the Gentiles 'to be mocked' (20:19), and on three occasions during the passion story, this prophecy comes true: the Roman soldiers and the chief priests mock the suffering and crucified Jesus (27:29, 31, 41). While the mocking of Herod leads to rage and murder, the reader will eventually discover that the mocking of Jesus will lead to his own death which will reverse the mockery: 'He saved others, let him save himself' (27:42). By not saving himself, as Herod attempts to do, he will save others, fulfilling the earlier prophecy of the angel to Joseph: 'You shall call his name Jesus, for he will save his people from their sins' (1:21). The mocking of Herod leads to murder; the mocking of Jesus will bring life.

---

40 A similar link between Jesus' sonship and the Exodus will be found in the baptism of Jesus (3:13-17). On this, see R.E. Brown, *Birth*, pp. 215-216. J.D. Kingsbury, *Matthew as Story*, pp. 43-44 rightly points out that 'the reader' is made aware of Jesus' sonship in the infancy story, while it is publicly proclaimed in 3:17.

The tragedy of the slaying of the children again fulfills the words of a prophet: 'A voice was heard in Ramah, wailing and loud lamentation, Rachel weeping for her children; she refused to be consoled, because they were no more' (v. 18).[41] The quotation of Jer 31:15 sheds light on Herod's action. Even this terrible event was predicted by the prophets. It is a part of God's strange ways. The ancestral mother of Israel, Rachel, weeps for her children.[42] Herod cannot be a true King of the Jews if he kills Israel's children because of Jesus. The King of Israel cannot reject the King of Israel.[43] However, the narrator has left Jesus in Egypt. There was another child whose birth had been marked by the slaying of innocent Hebrew children: Moses (see Ex 1:15-22).[44] The suggestion that a new Moses would come out of Egypt to form a new people of God, first made in the quotation of Hosea 11:1 in v. 15, is still present. It will be in the mind of the reader as Jesus ascends a mountain to teach his disciples that many of the things which had been said of old were now being brought to their perfection by his word: 'You have heard that it was said to the men of old ... but I say to you' (see 5:1-2, 17-48).[45]

41   On the complexities of the citation of Jeremiah 31:15 in Matthew 2:18, see R.E. Brown, *Birth*, pp. 221-223.

42   There are many difficulties over the placing of Ramah. The original prophecy locates it north-east of Jerusalem, on the way to Babylon, while Gen 35:19 and 48:7 led to a tradition which located the tomb of Rachel near Bethlehem. Matthew is following this Bethlehem tradition. On this, see U. Luz, *Matthew*, p. 147, note 27, and R. E. Brown, *Birth*, p. 205.

43   See U. Luz, *Matthew*, p. 147.

44   On this background, see W.D. Davies – D.C. Allison, *Saint Matthew*, pp. 264-265; E. Schweizer, *Matthew*, pp. 42-43.

45   While making these claims for the Matthean portrait of Jesus, I am aware that Jesus is not portrayed as 'another Moses'. The Matthean understanding of the relationship has been well described by W.D. Davies, *The Setting of the Sermon on the Mount* (Cambridge: University Press, 1963) p. 93: 'The

After the interlude which shows the true and the false King of Israel, the narrator recalls the flight into Egypt, but links all three final scenes by setting the time: 'when Herod died' (v. 19. See vv. 15; 16). The angel of the Lord commands Joseph, and the direct speech of the angel is again translated into action by the narrator's description of Joseph's actions in words which repeat the direct speech of the angel (vv. 20-21). Joseph's never-failing and radical response to the word of God throughout the narrative has by now become a *leit-motif*. Whatever he does corresponds to the plan of God. His obedience makes him a vital link in God's saving story.[46] As the major events in the story fulfil the promises of the word of God made through the prophets, the succession of events found within the narrative itself take place only because Joseph never questions the word of God revealed through his angel.

He is warned 'in a dream' that the new ruler, Archelaus, is a threat to the child and he withdraws to Galilee (v. 22). No doubt the author now has to deal with the question of Jesus' origins. He was known as Jesus of Nazareth, but the story so far could only make of him: Jesus of Bethlehem, or even Jesus of Egypt![47] The story now informs

strictly Mosaic traits in the figure of the Matthean Christ ... have been taken up into a deeper and higher context. He is not Moses come as Messiah, if we may so put it, so much as Messiah, Son of Man, Emmanuel, who has absorbed the Mosaic function'.

46 See D.B. Howell, *Matthew's Inclusive Story. A Study in the Narrative Rhetoric of the First Gospel* (JSNTSS 42; Sheffield: JSOT Press, 1990) pp. 116-120. Howell rightly uncovers a combination of acceptance/rejection and prediction/fulfillment in Matthew 1-2 (and beyond).

47 Indeed, there is an early Jewish polimic against Jesus which describes him as an Egyptian magician. For a collection of this evidence, see J.Z. Lauterbach, 'Jesus in the Talmud', in T. Weiss-Rosmarin, *Jewish Expressions on Jesus. An Anthology* (New York: KTAV, 1977) pp. 1-98.

the reader how he came to be known as Jesus 'of Nazareth', a little known Galilean village, never mentioned in the Old Testament, and hardly ever mentioned in other Jewish sources.[48] The theme of 'where from' is certainly present in vv. 19-23.

Nevertheless, the final citation from Scripture ensures that the question of Jesus' person and destiny as the fulfilment of God's prophetic promise is not lost from the reader's view. No longer does the narrator tell his reader that any single prophet spoke of Nazareth. His going to Nazareth fulfils 'the prophets'. Indeed there is difficulty in identifying a biblical source for the saying. It is a saying formed by several Old Testament motifs. 'He shall be called a Nazarene' refers, first of all, to the historical fact that he was called a Nazarene. But behind this description of Jesus stands the Jewish figure of the *nazir* (see Num 6:1-21, and then Judg 13:5, 7; 16:17): a holy man consecrated to God. Also involved is the Jewish hope that the Messiah would be a branch *(neser)* from the root of Jesse (see Is 11:1). Jesus is both. He is the Holy one, committed to God, and he is the promised Messiah, the product of the Davidic line, the branch from the root of Jesse.[49]

---

48 See R.E. Brown, *Birth*, pp. 207-208.
49 For a full discussion of these possibilities, see R.E. Brown, *Birth*, pp. 209-213. Brown rightly concludes: 'They are not mutually exclusive but reflect the allusive wealth of the term' (pp. 218-219). This also partly explains the plural 'prophets'. Thus also K. Kermode, 'Matthew', p. 396. U. Luz, *Matthew*, pp. 149-150, concludes that one should choose between the *nazir* of Judges 13:5, 7; 16:17 and the *neser* of Isaiah 11:1. He decides in favour of Isaiah 11:1. W.D. Davies – D.C. Allison, *Saint Matthew*, pp. 275-281, also decide for Isaiah 11:1, but only as a secondary allusion. The main allusion is to Isaiah 4:3, where Matthew has altered 'He will be called holy' to 'He will be called a Nazarene'.

CONCLUSION

The reader comes to the last line of the infancy story informed that Jesus fulfils the promises of the Old Testament yet introduces a new way in which God is with his people. The reader knows that Jesus is the Son of David, the Son of Abraham, the King of Israel, the Son of God, the new and perfect Moses, the Holy One of God, the messianic shoot from the stump of Jesse. Although a historical-critical analysis of the words of 2:23 alone may not produce all these claims for Jesus, the reader, on arrival at 2:23, is aware that the words, 'He shall be called a Nazarene', which lead into the life story of Jesus of Nazareth, imply them all.

The reader has experienced a narrative which tells of the author's convictions of who Jesus is, the fulfilment of God's plans as Son of God, Son of David and Son of Abraham. The reader is aware that God has directed history which has led to salvation (see 1:21), to the presence of God among us (see 1:23).[50] But the reader is also aware of the nature of the response required. The women in the genealogy, Joseph and the wise men in the story, have all pointed the way. God's designs may appear strange to the ways of the world. The coming of Jesus by means of a virgin birth is strange indeed. But an acceptance of God's ways leads humankind further towards the accomplishment of all that God has promised.

Wayne Booth may again be cited: 'Significant literature arouses suspense not about the "what" but about the

---

50 In his perceptive study of Matthew 1-2, B.B. Scott, 'The Birth', pp. 83-102, does not make enough God's role in the story. He admits that God is 'the text's ultimate ideological authority' (p. 90), but I hope to have shown that God is an active agent in the narrative, not just its ideological authority.

"how"'.[51] With Matthew's Gospel there are two 'hows'
to be answered. In the first place, how will the story of
Jesus correspond to the exalted claims made for him in
the infancy narrative: he is the perfection of the promises
of God? But also, how will the reader continue to be a
part of God's unfolding history, in imitation of the women
in the genealogy, Joseph and the wise men?

---

51 W. Booth, *Rhetoric*, p. 255. See also G. Watson, 'The Sense of a Beginning', *The Sewanee Review* 86 (1978) 548: 'The How, after all, concerns
the deepest texture of literature'.

4 | BEGINNING THE GOSPEL OF LUKE
LUKE 1:1-2:52

Unlike the Matthean story of the darkness of persecution, murder and flight (see Mt 2:1-23), in Luke 1-2 we read two annunciations (Lk 1:5-38), a meeting of two mothers (vv. 39-56), two births (1:57-2:21), a visit to the Temple (2:22-38), the loss of Jesus and his eventual rediscovery in the Temple (vv. 41-52). Only in Simeon's words to Jesus' Mother (esp. 2:34-35) and in the loss of the adolescent boy do shadows appear (esp. 2:48-51). For the rest, God's ways are done in peace and joy.

There are many characters in the Lukan narrative: Zechariah, Gabriel, Elizabeth, Mary, Joseph, Zechariah and Elizabeth's neighbours and kinsfolk, shepherds, an angel of the Lord, Simeon, Anna, the company from Nazareth travelling back from Jerusalem, among them Joseph and Mary's kinsfolk and acquaintances, the teachers in the Temple. The events of the narrative take place in established places (Nazareth, Bethlehem and Jerusalem) and at a given time, in the days of Herod, king of Judea (1:5), when Augustus was the Emperor and

Quirinius the governor of Syria (2:1-2). The association of John the Baptist's annunciation and birth with that of Jesus enriches the sequence of events.

These initial observations indicate that the experience of reading Luke 1-2 will be complex.[1] Compared to Matthew 1-2, there are more events and more characters involved in those events.[2] My reading will concentrate upon this latter issue: who are the protagonists in the first two chapters of the Gospel of Luke? Although present from the story of his birth (2:1-21), Jesus is not active until the final episode. The Lukan Christology certainly emerges in the infancy story, but is Luke 1-2 primarily about Jesus?[3]

TO BEGIN AT THE BEGINNING: Luke 1:1-4

Unlike all other Gospels, the Lukan narrator opens the story by directly addressing his reader, Theophilus

---

1   As R.C. Tannehill, *The Narrative Unity of Luke-Acts. A Literary Interpretation* (2 vols.; Philadelphia: Fortress Press, 1986-1990) Vol 1, p. 5, remarks: 'The text is like a rope with multiple strands'.

2   On the 'events' in narrative, see S. Chatman, *Story and Discourse*, pp. 45-84, and on characters as 'existents' in a narrative, see *ibid.*, pp. 107-138. See also M.A. Powell, *What Is Narrative Criticism?*, pp. 35-67.

3   The magisterial work of R.E. Brown, *Birth*, has correctly shifted interest in the infancy narratives away from history into the developing Christology of the early Church. Another work which exaggeratedly concentrates on the Christology of Luke 1-2, paying little attention to the role which God plays, is C.H. Talbert, *Reading Luke. A Literary and Theological Commentary on the Third Gospel* (New York: Crossroad, 1982) pp. 18-21, 31-34, 35-38. My study of Luke 1-2 attempts to show that Theology, i.e. an understanding of God, is Luke's major concern. In this I have been guided by the research of Mark Coleridge, at present in preparation for publication under the title *The Birth of the Lukan Narrative. Narrative as Christology in Luke 1-2*. I take this occasion to thank him for his gracious sharing of his work with me in Jerusalem in June-August of 1990. See also J.N. Aletti, *L'art de raconter Jésus Christ* (Paris: Seuil, 1989) pp. 63-85. Among the commentators, E. Schweizer, *The Good News according to Luke* (Atlanta: John Knox, 1984) pp. 15-67, is most sensitive to the Theology of the narrative.

(Lk 1:1-4).[4] By means of a contrived literary piece, one long sentence, Luke links the past story of Jesus with his present readership. Although there are various other Lukan introductions throughout his two-volume work (see especially Lk 3:1-2; Acts 1:1-2), these passages 'resemble it in style but do not match it in perfection'.[5] Comparison with classical prefaces from antiquity show that Luke has deliberately imitated an established classical style.[6]

The narrative which follows in 1:5-2:52 does not continue the elegant Greek of the preface, but is closer to the Greek of the LXX.[7] The reader experiences a work of literary merit, written by an author who can adapt his Greek to a variety of styles, addressed to a Gentile audience.[8] But there is more. The reader also becomes aware that there were other 'narratives' (v. 1: *diêgêsin*) about

---

4   As well as the commentaries, for what follows see especially R.J. Dillon, 'Previewing Luke's Project from His Prologue (Luke 1:1-4)', *CBQ* 43 (1981) 205-227. See also P.S. Minear, 'Dear Theo. The Kerygmatic Intention and Claim of the Book of Acts', *Int* 27 (1973) 131-150; R.C. Tannehill, *Narrative Unity*, Vol 1, pp. 9-12; G. Schneider, *Das Evangelium nach Lukas. Kapitel 1-10* (ÖTB 3/1; Gütersloh/Würzburg: Gerd Mohn/Echter, 1977) pp. 37-41.

5   J.A. Fitzmyer, *The Gospel According to Luke I-IX* (AB 28; Garden City: Doubleday, 1981) p. 288.

6   See L. Alexander, 'Luke's Preface in the Context of Greek Preface-Writing', *NovT* 28 (1986) 48-74. For a list of parallel prefaces, and a discussion of the component elements, see C.F. Evans, *Saint Luke* (TPINTC; Philadelphia: Trinity Press International, 1990) pp. 115-119.

7   As E. Laverdiere, *Luke* (NTM 5; Wilmington: Michael Glazier, 1980) p. 11, writes: 'The passage from one to the other is sudden and the contrast unmistakable, as though one had moved from Thucydides to the Septuagint'.

8   While there is no reason to doubt that there was a 'Theophilus', this intended audience is outside our control. The name indicates that the work is directed to a Gentile readership, although it could be applied to a Jew. Thus the NRSV's affirmation 'probably a Roman of high rank' (p. 76NT) assumes too much. On Theophilus, see J.A. Fitzmyer, *Luke*, pp. 299-230; J.N. Aletti, *L'art*, pp. 223-224. On Luke's use of Greek, see N. Turner, 'The Style of Luke-Acts', in J.H. Moulton – N. Turner (ed.), *A Grammar of the Greek New Testament* (Edinburgh: T. & T. Clark, 1976) Vol 4, pp. 45-63.

events (v. 1: *pragmata*) from the life of Jesus which preceded the one about to be read.

However, the author is not totally satisfied with them.
In order to give depth and certainty (v. 4: *asphaleian*) to
an instruction already received (v. 4: *katêchêthês logôn*) the
author, a third generation Christian, has joined a line of
witnesses which ran from Jesus to disciples who became
ministers and witnesses of the word (v. 2: 'those who from
the beginning were eyewitnesses and ministers of the word'
[*autoptai kai hupêretai genomenoi tou logou*]) to the Lukan
Churches (v. 2: 'delivered to us' [*paredosan hêmin*]). He
now wishes to pass on to a later generation of communities in the Gentile mission,[9] an understanding of the
events of the life of Jesus, by writing a carefully (v. 3:
akribôs) planned orderly account of everything (v. 3: *pasin*),
'from the beginnings' of the Christian story (v. 2: *ap'archês*)
down to his own time.

A theological program has been outlined. The reader
has begun a narrative written with a deliberate design
(v. 3: 'an orderly account' [*kathêxês*]): to comfort and guide
by linking him or her back to the promises made at the
beginning of the Christian movement. But the present
experience of the reader is the fulfillment of what was
promised at the beginning (v. 1: 'the things which have
been accomplished [*peplêrophorêmôn*] among us').[10] Of

---

9 On this, see R.J. Karris, 'Missionary Communities: A New Paradigm for
   the Study of Luke-Acts', *CBQ* 41 (1979) 80-97.
10 See R.C. Tannehill, *Narrative Unity*, Vol 1, p. 10: 'For some reason narrating
   "in order" should lead to "assurance". It should have a convincing and
   faith-supporting function'. See D.L. Tiede, *Prophecy and History in Luke-
   Acts* (Philadelphia: Fortress Press, 1980). See also D. Juel, *Luke-Acts. The
   Promise of History* (Atlanta: John Knox Press, 1983). On 1:1-4, see pp.
   113-123.

this the reader will eventually be made certain. If this does not happen, then the author will have failed.[11]

THE SHAPE OF LUKE 1:5-2:52

The most obvious element in the overall shape of Luke 1:5-2:52 is the repetitive pattern of annunciation and birth stories.[12] The annunciation of John the Baptist (1:5-25) and of Jesus (1:26-38) is told in succession. Because they are both modelled upon the Old Testament pattern of an annunciation, they are structurally close.[13] After the encounter between the two mothers (1:39-56), the story of the Baptist and the story of Jesus are again related through the telling and retelling of their birth, circumcision and naming (John the Baptist: 1:57-80; Jesus: 2:1-21). The parallels between the birth stories, however, are not as close as those of the annunciation stories, simply because the former are not based on an Old Testament pattern.[14]

The parallel telling of the annunciation and the birth of John the Baptist and Jesus has led to a widespread understanding of Luke 1-2 as a diptych: a narrative composed around these two corresponding stories.[15] The

---

11 J.N. Aletti, *L'art*, 217-233, closes his book on Luke's narrative with a study of 1:1-4 as a verification of the results of his analysis of the Gospel's narration.
12 I am presuming that Luke 1-2 form the prologue to the Gospel of Luke. C.H. Talbert, *Literary Patterns, Theological Themes and the Genre of Luke-Acts* (SBLMS 20; Missoula: Scholars Press, 1974) pp. 43-48 and *Reading Luke*, pp. 15-17, suggests that 1:5-4:15 form a unit. He is followed by J.N. Aletti, *L'art*, pp. 80-82.
13 On the annunciation pattern, see R.E. Brown, *Birth*, pp. 292-298.
14 See R.E. Brown, *Birth*, p. 409. G. Schneider, *Lukas*, p. 65.
15 For a survey, see R.E. Brown, *Birth*, pp. 248-253; J.A. Fitzmyer, *Luke I-IX*, pp. 313-315; E. Laverdiere, *Luke*, p. 13; O.C. Edwards, *Luke's Story of Jesus* (Philadelphia: Fortress Press, 1981) pp. 17-28. For my own earlier suggestions along these lines, see F.J. Moloney, 'The infancy narratives in Luke', in H. McGinlay (ed.), *The Year of Luke* (Melbourne: Desbooks/JBCE, 1982) pp. 4-9.

problem with such literary shapes is that readers don't read like that! There is an undeniable repetition of annunciation and birth stories, but they are read successively, not in parallel.[16]

The various parts of the narrative are obvious, but how do they relate to one another? Insisting upon the temporal, rather than the spatial, as the major element in the reading process, I propose the following narrative shape:

1. **1:5-25:** The annunciation of John the Baptist to Zechariah sets the agenda: God, the chief character in the story, communicates his designs for the human story. The reader is not told of Zechariah's internal acceptance or refusal of God's promise. He is struck dumb, but he returns home and his wife conceives.

2. **1:26-38:** The annunciation of Jesus to Mary continues the agenda of the chief character. Again without actively entering the story, God makes his designs known to Mary through Gabriel. The reader is introduced to the internal process of Mary's gradual coming to identify God at the centre of her future (v. 38).

3. **1:39-56:** The woman who became a mother as a result of the first annunciation story salutes the mother from the second annunciation story.

16 Only the critical reader, with the aid of modern printing techniques, can approach the text in this way. It was not the case with an ancient author writing on papyrus. As C.F. Evans, *Saint Luke*, p. 139, remarks: 'Luke has used these units to tell an almost continuous story with a considerable amount of movement and characterization'. R.C. Tannehill, *Literary Unity*, pp. 15-20, argues that 'the repetitive pattern ... does not compete with but rather contributes to the forward movement of the story' (p. 17). See also J. Drury, 'Luke' in *The Literary Guide*, pp. 418-419.

4. **1:57-80:** The promise of the first annunciation is partially fulfilled. The annunciation of John the Baptist led to dumbness and a conception. The conception leads to birth. The naming of the child, in total obedience to the word of God, leads to speech.

5. **2:1-21:** The promised Davidic Saviour who is Christ the Lord (v. 11) is born in a manger and wrapped in swaddling cloths (vv. 7, 12, 16). God's promises are again partially fulfilled. The birth of the child is surrounded by events which keep God at the centre of the story, even though God does not appear.

6. **2:22-40:** In the Jerusalem Temple two righteous Old Testament figures, Simeon and Anna, recognise the turning point of the ages.

7. **2:41-52:** For the first time in the narrative, Jesus is the chief protagonist. Looking back to all that has happened thus far as the plan of God, he now tells his wondering parents that his role is to be about the affairs of his Father.

The narrative concentrates its attention upon the two sides of a meeting between heaven and earth: the initiative of God, through his agents, and the response of those whom God visits. In obedience to the command of the angel (see 1:31) the name 'Jesus' is given in 2:21, and used of him after that moment (2:27, 43, 52), but all other references to the child born of Mary look to the future.[17] He does not play an active role until the final scene (2:41-52) where he both responds to the action of God, and embodies the visitation of God (2:49).

---

17 For an analysis of all the references to Jesus in Luke 1-2, see J.N. Aletti, *L'art*, pp. 75-78.

READING THE NARRATIVE[18]

1. Reading Luke 1:5-25

The narrative opens with a terse description of the time: in the days of Herod; the characters: Zechariah the priest, Elizabeth of the daughters of Aaron; and their situation: they were righteous before God, but are now elderly and without a child (vv. 5-7). Firmly fixed in time and in a given situation, their relationship to the God of Israel is the dominant feature of their lives (v. 6).[19] The narrator next describes Zechariah's call to duty in the Temple. The fact that 'it fell to him by lot' is a first hint to the reader that God is involved in Zechariah's presence in the Temple. The narrator informs the reader that 'the whole multitude of the people' were 'outside'. Israel is present, God-directed in its prayer.

In this situation 'an angel of the Lord' appears. God is present, but not in person. God acts through his agent – the angel of the Lord. The pattern of an Old Testament annunciation story has determined the flow of events

---

18 Given the length of the Lukan infancy narrative I will only dwell on the main thrust of each section to present my overall impression of the narration. For more detailed exegetical questions, I refer the reader to the commentaries, especially those of R.E. Brown, J.A. Fitzmyer and I.H. Marshall, *The Gospel of Luke. A Commentary on the Greeek Text* (NIGTC; Exeter: Paternoster Press, 1978) pp. 45-130. Most sections of the narrative conclude with formulae of growth or departure (see 1:38c, 56, 80; 2:21, 39-40, 52). I will not comment upon this feature.

19 See R.E. Brown, *Birth*, p. 268: 'Combining priestly origins and blameless observance of the Law, Zechariah and Elizabeth were for Luke the representatives of the best in the religion of Israel'. Despite this comment, Brown does not make enough of their relationship to God in his discussion of vv. 5-7 (see pp. 265-269). R.C. Tannehill, *Literary Unity*, pp. 17-19, shows that Luke 1-2 'is permeated with the Old Testament hope and celebrates its fulfilment' (p. 18).

which follow,[20] but the author communicates his unique point of view by the content of those events. The angel's response to Zechariah's fear is to assure him 'your prayer is heard' (v. 13).

The use of the divine passive ('is heard' [*eisêkouthê*]) keeps God at the centre of the story.[21] The future birth of a son is the result of God's intervention into the story of Zechariah and Elizabeth, demanding obedience: 'you shall call his name John' (v. 13). A rhythm has been established: God enters the human story, and asks that human beings respond to his intervention. The couple who have always walked according to the commandmants of the Lord (see v. 6) are being challenged to recognise that their traditional God is now acting in their life in a new way.

The description of the child (vv. 14-17) will only be partially fulfilled within the infancy narrative: 'you will have joy and gladness and many will have joy at his birth' (v. 14. See 1:57-58). The reader must wait for his ministry before the rest of the description is fulfilled (see 3:1-20).[22] However, the reader is informed from John's annunciation that his role is to point beyond himself 'to turn many of the sons of Israel to the Lord their God' (v. 16) and 'to make ready for the Lord a people prepared' (v. 17). As the angel is an agent who moves from heaven to earth,

20 See Gen 16:7-13 (annunciation of Ishmael), Gen 17:1-3, 15-21; 18:1-2, 10-15 (Isaac) and Judges 13:2-23 (Samson). On this pattern, see R.E. Brown, *Birth*, pp. 156-159.
21 See ZBG, para. 236.
22 On this, see C.H. Talbert, *Reading Luke*, pp. 27-30; J.A. Fitzmyer, 'The Lucan Picture of John the Baptist as Precursor of the Lord', in *Luke the Theologian. Aspects of His Teaching* (London: Geoffrey Chapman, 1989) pp. 86-116.

John is to be an agent of God on earth, among 'the people of Israel'.[23]

It would be quite reasonable for Zechariah to ask how such a conception could take place, given the age of both himself and his wife. But he does not ask 'how can this be' (see the question of Mary in 1:34), but 'How shall I know this?' (*kata ti gnôsomai touto;*. See Gen 15:8).[24] It is not a question which expresses wonder at the action of God, but a question which asks how he can be sure that such things will happen to him. He attempts to usurp the initiative which belongs to God alone when heaven meets earth.[25] The authority of the angel Gabriel who stands in the presence of God (v. 19. See Dan 7:16; 9:16; 8:21) maintains both the absence and yet the presence of a transcendent God. It is God who has spoken through the words of the angel. As such, they will bear fruit, but the speech of Zechariah will cease (vv. 19b-20).

As Zechariah delays, 'the people' are no longer at prayer. They begin to wonder (v. 21). Their wonder will increase as the narrative unfolds (see 1:65-66; 2:18). When Zechariah finally emerges and they are unable to speak with him, they 'perceived that he had seen a vision in the Temple'. There is no indication that they do anything more than wonder. While God has been present in the events which have touched the life of Zechariah, 'the people' who began in prayer (see v. 10) now only wonder.

23 Although 'the Lord' in the use of Isaiah 40:3 in Mark 1:3 applies to Jesus, the expression in Luke 1:17 refers to God. This is demanded by the parallel use of 'the Lord their God' in v. 16 and 'the Lord' in v. 17. See J.A. Fitzmyer, *Luke I-IX*, p. 327.
24 On the parallels between the annunciation to Zechariah and the situation of Abraham and Sarah, see J.N. Aletti, *L'art*, pp. 67-69.
25 Against R.E. Brown, *Birth*, p. 280, (among many) who sees little difference between this question and Mary's question in v. 34.

The story hastens to a conclusion.[26] Zechariah concludes his period of service, returns home and Elizabeth conceives. Already within this narrative the promise of God, made through the angel Gabriel, is being fulfilled. Elizabeth immediately recognises that God has visited her: 'This is what the Lord has done to me when he looked favorably on me' (v. 25).

The protagonists in the story are God, who justifiably can never appear in person, but only through his angel,[27] and Zechariah, who fails to accept the absolute authority of God when heaven meets earth. Surrounding these two major characters are 'all the people' who move from prayer to human wonder, and Elizabeth who recognises that God has visited her.

2. Reading Luke 1:26-38

The scene opens with a reminiscence of the experience of Elizabeth's hiding herself *for five months* in 1:24. We now read: '*In the sixth month* the angel Gabriel was sent by God' (1:26). The angel comes 'to a virgin'. Not only has a link been made back to the preceding narrative, but the characters of the present action have been fully introduced: the angel from God and a virgin named Mary. The term *parthenos* appears twice in v. 27. This is significant, as it is the author's way of indicating that Mary was a virgin at the conception of Jesus.[28] Although the

---

26 On the narrator's control of the speed of a narrative, see G. Genette, *Narrative Discourse*, pp. 33-160.
27 God is the prime mover and protagonist of the narrative. God is mentioned as *theos* 20 times in Luke 1-2, but he never appears or speaks. God's various messengers are seen and heard. See J.N. Aletti, *L'art*, pp. 70-71.
28 On the historical problem of the virginal conception, see R.E. Brown, *Birth*, pp. 517-533, and C.F. Evans, *Saint Luke*, pp. 154-158.

question of Mary's virginity became very important in the later life and preaching of the Church, her physical state at the conception of Jesus is not about the *virtue of Mary* but about the *origins* of the virgin's child.[29] The way is being cleared for the introduction of the major character in the action: God, who again speaks through his agent.

The virgin is described as 'betrothed to a man whose name was Joseph' (v. 27). Mary has not yet been led to the house of Joseph, but her being betrothed to a man explicitly named as 'of the house of David' already makes her his 'wife'.[30] Gabriel greets the young woman with an expression that is difficult to render precisely: *chaire kecharitômenê*. Both verbs come from the same basic root which expresses joy.[31] One verb greets Mary, and the other is used in a perfect passive form to describe her as one to whom God has freely given his gifts: 'Rejoice, O highly favoured one!'. Gabriel's salutation indicates the absolute initiative of God in all that is happening. God did not *have* to choose Mary – God acts out of his freedom. Thus the reader is able to understand the power of the angel's following affirmation: 'the Lord is with you'. This expression, taken from the Old Testament (see

---

29 The meaning of Mary's virginity should be seen in the light of the oriental and biblical world's negative view of such a state. It is a form of *kenosis*, i.e., a radical openness to God. On this, see L. Boff, *The Maternal Face of God. The Feminine and Its Religious Expressions* (San Francisco: Harper & Row, 1987) pp. 137-139; F.J. Moloney, *Mary Woman and Mother* (Homebush: St Paul Publications, 1988) pp. 17-18.

30 See R.E. Brown, *Birth*, pp. 123-124 and C.F. Evans, *Saint Luke*, pp. 159-160, for a synthesis of these practices. For more detail, see J. Jeremias, *Jerusalem in the Time of Jesus* (London: SCM Press, 1969) pp. 364-368.

31 See X. Jacques, *List of New Testament Words Sharing Common Elements* (Rome: Biblical Institute Press, 1969) p. 120.

Gen 26:24; 28:15; Ex 3:12; Judg 6:12; Jer 1:8, 19; 15:20),[32]
is an assurance that no matter what might befall her, and
no matter what might be thought or said of her, God's
plans for her will be effectively realised.

Mary's being troubled, 'considering in her mind what
sort of greeting this might be' (v. 29), is understandable.[33]
The reader finds that Mary's *first* reaction is one of human
puzzlement and confusion. She is unable to utter a single
word in her shock and consternation. The angel calms
her fears explaining: 'You have found favour with God'
(v. 30). An expression is used which always indicates the
free and gracious choice of YHWH, who favours particular women and men (see, for example, Gen 6:8; Judg 6:17;
I Sam 1:18; II Sam 15:25). The stress is still upon the
mystery of a God who invites a human being to be part
of his design.

The reader discovers that the child to be born of the
virgin will fulfill Jewish messianic hopes:

He will be great,
and will be called the son of the Most High,
and the Lord God will give to him
the throne of his ancestor David.
He will reign over the house of Jacob forever,
and of his kingdom there will be no end (vv. 32-33).

All these promises can be found in the Jewish hopes for
their coming Messiah, including 'the son of the Most

32 See W.C. van Unnik, '*Dominus Vobiscum:* The Background of a Liturgical
    Formula', in *New Testament Essays. Studies in Memory of Thomas Walter
    Manson 1893 – 1958* (Manchester: University Press, 1959) pp. 276-286 for
    a list of Old Testament and Jewish sources where the expression is used.
    The article runs from pp. 270-305.
33 It is, of course, also part of the annunciation pattern.

High'.[34] Mary is told that she will be the mother of the expected Messiah. Although an extraordinary privilege is bestowed upon her through the initiative of God, in the context of the messianic expectation of the first century, it is within the realms of the *expected* and the *humanly possible*.

Mary questions this possibility (v. 34). While the author uses the literary pattern of an annunciation gradually to reveal God's initiative, he also shows his reader a 'journey of faith' in Mary's response. While the greeting of the angel led to puzzlement and fear (v. 29), Mary now poses a perfectly reasonable question. She has moved from *astonishment to reason*. Zechariah asked how he could know of God's action (1:18); Mary asks how she can conceive, given her physical situation: 'How can this be, since I am not knowing a man' (v. 34). She is a virgin, and does not have a sexual relationship with Joseph. She is not seeking control; she simply asks how such wonders can happen. Mary has reacted with a reasonable question. The author shows a development in Mary's response.

While vv. 32-33 spoke of a messianic king, and led to the query of v. 34, v. 35 speaks of the conception and the child in a way which surpasses Jewish religious and cultural expectations:

> The Holy Spirit will come upon you,
> and the power of the Most High will overshadow you;
> therefore the child to be born will be holy;
> he will be called Son of God (v. 35).

---

34 See, on this, H. Cazelles, *Le Messie de la Bible* (Série Jésus et Jésus Christ; Paris: Desclée, 1978). On the Jewish use of 'son of the Most High' as a messianic term (based on Ps 2:7 and 2 Sam 7:14), see B.J. Byrne, *'Sons of God — Seed of Abraham'*, pp. 9-78.

The 'sign' of Elizabeth is given (v. 36). If Mary is faced with a promise that she will be the virgin mother of the Son of God which she could regard as 'impossible', then the sign given to her is the maternity of her elderly kins-woman – a further 'impossibility'. In explanation of what is happening to *both* women, the angel announces in v. 37: 'For nothing will be impossible with God'. All that the reader has read in 1:5-36 is impossible, yet with God nothing is impossible. Although God has never 'spoken' directly to the participants in the events taking place, divine initiative and freedom dominate the narrative.[35]

The text is not *primarily* about Mary, but about the transforming power of a God whose design causes heaven to touch earth. It is the response of Mary to his design which gives her a special place in the story of God's action in the history of women and men:

> Here am I, the servant of the Lord;
> let it be with me according to your word (v. 38).

The appearance of the angel has led to an amazed puzzlement (v. 29); the annunciation of the birth of the long-awaited Messiah has led to a perfectly logical objection (v. 34). Now Mary, informed that she has been caught up into a plan of God that reaches outside all human measurement and control, is being asked to give herself and her future history to 'the Holy Spirit ... the power of the Most High'. She commits herself to the word and

---

35 The God of the Lukan infancy narrative is very different from the God of Old Testament narrative. In the Old Testament God may appear very rarely, but speaks a great deal. On this, see M. Sternberg, *The Poetics of Biblical Narrative*, pp. 99-128. Sternberg notes: 'God himself must figure as the busiest agent, indeed superagent, bringing his might to bear on the world to make history and flaunting it to the world to publish authority' (p. 102).

ways of God (v. 38). The description of the child as the
fulfilment of Israel's messianic hopes and the Son of God
(v. 35) provides the reader with important information
about the future role of Jesus. However, God (through
his angel) and Mary have been at the centre of the action, not the child who is yet to be born. The story time
is dominated by God and Mary. The predictions about
Jesus' future (prolepses) are not yet part of the story. They
belong to narrative time.

3. Reading Luke 1:39-56

Two mothers meet.[36] In response to the information
given to her by the angel (see v. 36), Mary travels to 'a
city of Judah', enters Zechariah's house and greets
Elizabeth (vv. 39-41). Her greeting elicits two responses,
both of which are directed to Mary. The babe leaps in
Elizabeth's womb, and she is filled with the Holy Spirit.
Elizabeth recognises the blessedness of her younger kins-
woman and of her child and directs the wonder entirely
to Mary as 'the Mother of my Lord'. Similarly, the quick-
ening of Elizabeth's child in her womb results from Mary's
greeting. The unborn John does not salute the unborn
Jesus, as is often claimed.[37] There is no mention of this
in the text. The reason for the greeting continues what

---

36 C.F. Evans, *Saint Luke*, p. 168, correctly remarks: 'It is the linchpin from
   both the literary and theological point of view of the narratives of the con-
   ceptions and births of John and Jesus'. See also G. Schneider, *Lukas*, p. 44.
   For a different opinion, see J.A. Fitzmyer, *Luke I-IX*, p. 314. Fitzmyer regards
   it as a complementary scene corresponding to 2:41-52.
37 See, for example, R.E. Brown, *Birth*, p. 341: 'Now JBap begins to prophesy
   in the womb by jumping with gladness (41, 44b) − a gladness that hails
   the advent of the messianic age'. See also J.A. Fitzmyer, *Luke I-IX*,
   pp. 357-358; E. Schweizer, *Luke*, p. 358.

the reader has already learnt from 1:26-38: 'Blessed is she who believed that there would be a fulfilment of what was spoken to her by the Lord' (v. 45). The christological theme involved in the recognition of Mary's child as 'my Lord' is subordinated to the recognition of the action of God through Mary, who has laid herself open to his word.

Mary's response in the *Magnificat* (vv. 46-55) does not mention the child she is carrying.[38] She cries out her praise of the Lord, God her Saviour who has regarded the low estate of his servant (vv. 46-47a).[39] Not only Elizabeth, but all generations will call her blessed because 'the Mighty One has done great things for me' (v. 48b-49). The canticle looks to the past, to YHWH's presence to those of low degree throughout the history of his people. Mary's blessedness places her within a long history of YHWH's promises to Abraham and his posterity (vv. 50-55). But this promise will not end with her. It is 'from generation to generation' (v. 50), 'for ever' (v. 55). All readers can be part of the story of God's entry into the human story, raising up the lowly and setting the downtrodden free. The *Magnificat* is not about Mary or Jesus. 'Mary in the Magnificat sets her personal destiny in the context of the ultimate purposes of God for Israel'.[40] It is about God's way with the human story.

---

38 Accepting, with the majority of commentators, that Mary and not Elizabeth utters the *Magnificat*. For the discussion, see R.E. Brown, *Birth*, pp. 334-336.
39 Her virginity is a mark of her low estate. See above, note 29.
40 C.F. Evans, *Saint Luke*, p. 168. See especially R.C. Tannehill, *Narrative Unity*, pp. 26-32, For literature on the *Magnificat* see R.E. Brown, *Birth*, pp. 365-366; J.A. Fitzmyer, *Luke I-IX*, pp. 370-371. See especially, R.C. Tannehill, 'The Magnificat as Poem', *JBL* 93 (1974) 263-275; J. Dupont, 'Le Magnificat comme discours sur Dieu', *NRT* 102 (1980) 321-343.

The central characters in the story of the Visitation, Mary and Elizabeth, both point beyond themselves and their experiences to the action of God. Elizabeth and her child rejoice because Mary has believed in the fulfilment of God's word. Mary sings God's praises because God always has, and always will, raise up the lowly and put down the mighty. Her commitment to his word assures her blessedness (v. 48), but the initiative is always with God: 'The Mighty One has done great things for me, and holy is his name' (v. 49).

4. Reading Luke 1:57-80

The promise made to Zechariah was already partially fulfilled within the narrative of the annunciation. Elizabeth conceived (1:24). Now she gives birth, and her neighbours and kinsfolk recognise that 'the Lord had shown great mercy to her' (v. 58). However their rejoicing in what God has done for Elizabeth does not match either Mary's or Elizabeth's recognition of the action of God. The narrator continually uses the third person plural to refer back to the neighbours and kinsfolk: *they* came to circumcise the child (v. 59a); *they* insist that the child be called Zechariah (v. 59b); *they* object to the name 'John' (v. 61), *they* made signs to the father (v. 62), *they* all marvelled (v. 63). The narrator systematically presents the neighbours as attempting to impose their will.

There are two parties in a debate. On the one hand those who oppose God's designs, known only by Zechariah, Elizabeth and the reader, attempt to impose accepted tradition: calling the child by a family name. On the other, Elizabeth and Zechariah accept unconditionally the command of the angel of God. Gabriel had commanded: 'You

shall call his name John' (v. 13). Elizabeth tells her kinsfolk: 'He shall be called John' (v. 60)[41] and Zechariah
writes: 'His name is John' (v. 62). As the conception of
v. 24 led to the birth of v. 57, so now Zechariah's naming
of the child reverses his earlier desire to control the situation (see v. 18). His openness to the word of God's angel
(see v. 13) leads to speech, reversing Zechariah's dumbness (see v. 20). Although it has taken him longer, Zechariah's response to God's word now matches that of Mary
(see v. 38) and of Elizabeth (see vv. 45, 60).

The narrator does not immediately report what Zechariah said but returns to the neighbours. Fear comes upon
them, and these things are talked about through the hill
country of Judea. There is an awareness of the presence
of God in the events they have witnessed, but they are
unable to comprehend. The wonder associated with
Zechariah's dumbness as he came out of the Temple (see
1:21) is repeated. For this reason they lay the events up
in their hearts, waiting for a future moment when the
mysterious ways of God might be further revealed in the
life story of the child. The reader, although better informed than they are, joins the neighbours as they
ask: 'What then will this child become?' (v. 66). John's
future ministry lies beyond the limits of the present
narrative.

41 Critics often ask how Elizabeth knows the name, given the fact that Zechariah
was dumb. Such questions are of little interest to the author who here lines
up those who accept God's commands against those who do not. As R.E.
Brown, *Birth*, p. 369, comments: 'The reader is probably meant to think
that Elizabeth's decision was a spontaneous and marvellous confirmation
of God's plan'. However, if Zechariah was able to write the name for his
kinsfolk, he could have also done so privately for Elizabeth. Brown *(ibid.)*
rightly regards these specualtions as 'banal'. See, however, I.H. Marshall,
Luke, p. 88.

The reader, but not the neighbours, is further instructed through the *Benedictus* of the Spirit-filled Zechariah. While the *Magnificat* looked back upon the history of God's people, and explained the events of the present story in terms of the past, the *Benedictus* looks both backward and forward. The narrator informs the reader that Zechariah 'prophesied' *(epropheteusen)*. Once again God is at centre-stage throughout the canticle. Zechariah praises the Lord God of Israel, who has visited and redeemed his people (v. 67). The visitation of God provides liberation and salvation, fulfilling the promises of old (v. 70), the realisation of the faithful remembering of the covenant made with the fathers (v. 72), the oath sworn to Abraham (v. 73). But the visitation of God calls for a response: 'that we ... might serve him without fear, in holiness and righteousness before him all the days of our life' (vv. 74-75). This response has already been evidenced for the reader in the stories of Mary, Elizabeth and Zechariah.

The Baptist's future mission, again in fulfilment of the indications of the angel of God (see vv. 15-17), is described (vv. 76-77), but the canticle concludes with a further reflection on the visitation of God, bringing light to those who sit in darkness, guiding them into the way of peace (v. 80).[42] The *Benedictus* points the reader more firmly towards the coming Messiah and his Precursor, but God's purpose still dominates the narrative.[43]

---

42 See R.C. Tannehill, *Narrative Unity*, p. 33: 'The words addressed specifically to the baby John in 1:76-77 summarize the message of the angel about John in 1:17 ... The rest of the Benedictus does not refer specifically to John but celebrates God's act of salvation of which John will be a part'.

43 See R.C. Tannehill, *Narrative Unity*, pp. 32-38. For studies of the *Benedictus*, see J.A. Fitzmyer, *Luke I-IX*, pp. 370, 390.

Zechariah's canticle fits snugly into a story of God's visitation and the human response. 'By the tender mercy of our God, the dawn from on high will break upon us' (v. 78). Such tender mercy has been shown to the aged Zechariah, but absolute obedience has been demanded from him. Although he originally faltered, Zechariah has accepted that his name is 'John' (v. 63), his tongue has been loosened, and his first words bless the God of Israel who has visited his people.[44]

5. Reading Luke 2:1-21

In a descending order of importance, the reader is introduced to the greatest authority in the world, the author of the *Pax Romana* (v. 1: Caesar Augustus), to his envoy (v. 2: Quirinius) and finally to Joseph, Mary and a child born on a journey (vv. 4-7). The reader knows that the real author of peace is not Augustus, but God, who guides our feet into the way of peace (see 1:80), as he also knows that the child born to Mary is the Son of God (see v. 35).[45] Swaddled, as Solomon was swaddled (vv. 7, 12. See Wis 7:4-5), lain in a manger so that Israel might come to know its Master (vv. 7, 12, 16. See Is 1:2-3), this son of David (v. 4), Son of God (1:35) can find no place of rest. He is born on a journey for a journey.[46] Jesus has entered history, but not the narration. The reader is

---

44 On the importance of the theme of 'visitation' in the *Benedictus*, see R.C. Tannehill, *Narrative Unity*, p. 36.

45 See D. Juel, *Luke-Acts*, p. 19. On the historical problems, see R.E. Brown, *Birth*, pp. 547-556; C.F. Evans, *Saint Luke*, pp. 189-195.

46 I am unable to develop this theme here. The birth of Jesus adumbrates the journey theme which is important to Luke-Acts. On this, see F.J. Moloney, *The Living Voice*, pp. 67-92.

laconically told of the birth of Jesus, but the child plays
no active role in the story.

Shepherds, not highly regarded by the religiously pure
in Israel, receive a message of a babe wrapped in swaddling cloths and lying in a manger (v. 12) who will bring
peace to those blessed by the good gifts of God (v. 14).
An angel of the Lord tells them of the birth of a Davidic
Messiah (vv. 9-12), and heavenly hosts rejoice because God
has brought peace to earth (vv. 13-14). It is not the child
who dominates the scene, but God. The reader has been
told that heaven has touched earth, and that God will
bring the peace which God alone can give 'to those
favoured (by Him)' (v. 14).[47]

The shepherds go to Mary and the child, in obedience
to the command of the angel, and in recognition that the
Lord has made known these things to them. They make
known the things that had been said of the child (vv. 15-17).
The narrator closes this part of the story by reporting
three reactions to the events narrated. 'All who heard' what
the shepherds made known simply wonder (v. 18). A similar reaction accompanied the peoples' response to Zechariah's dumbness (1:21) and the naming of John (1:65-66).
The shepherds return to their fields, glorifying God, never
to appear in the story again (v. 20). 'But Mary kept all
these things, treasuring them in her heart' (v. 19).

The report of the events surrounding the naming of
the Baptist had led some to treasure them in their heart
(see 1:66). So also does Mary at the birth of her Son.
Like many characters from the story of Israel, she is unable

this, see R.E. Brown, *Birth*, pp. 403-404. See also J.A. Fitzmyer, *Luke*
p. 410-412.

to understand what God has done in and through her. Thus, she takes these mysteries into the depths of her being, once again open to the action of God in her life, cost her what it may (see Gen 37:11; 1 Sam 2:13; Mal 2:2; Sir 39:1-3; Prov 31; Ps 119:11; Dan 1:8; 4:28; 7:28).

The story of Jesus' birth is dominated by the action of God. Emperors, envoys and bystanders who hear the report of the shepherds play no part in God's entry into the human story. The shepherds respond to all that is asked of them, and they exit from the story praising God. At the end of the story Mary reappears. She is still portrayed as open to God's action which, as in the annunciation story, is beyond anything she could hope to understand or control.

6. Reading Luke 2:22-38

In accordance with the Law, Jesus is brought to the Temple for the purification and the offering of sacrifice (vv. 22-24). The world and the ways of Israel are present to the reader, and Simeon is introduced into this setting. Righteous, devout, open to the Holy Spirit, looking for the consolation of Israel and promised that he would see the Christ, he takes the child in his arms (vv. 25-26). In the name of all that has gone before he welcomes the turning point of the ages. This is the theme of the *Nunc dimittis* (vv. 29-32) and Simeon's oracle (vv. 34-35).[48]

It is not Simeon's personal history which is reflected in 'Master, now you are dismissing your servant in peace, according to your word' (v. 29). The whole of the old

---

48 See R.C. Tannehill, *Narrative Unity*, pp. 38-44.

economy says farewell, welcoming the salvation prepared from all time for all people: both Israel and the Gentiles (vv. 30-32). Simeon is not an elderly holy man who happens to be in the Temple on that day. Full of the Spirit, he represents all that has gone before as he takes his leave. God's history has reached its turning point.

As the father and mother of Jesus wonder at such words Simeon continues: 'This child is destined for the falling and the rising of many in Israel, and to be a sign that will be opposed so that the inner thoughts of many will be revealed – and a sword will pierce your own soul too' (vv. 34-35). The reader meets the words 'falling and rising' in that order. The words of Simeon introduce narrative time (a prolepsis) to tell the reader that while some Jews will accept Jesus, the majority will refuse to listen. Mary is presented as a part of this experience, but a different image is used. No longer does Simeon speak of 'falling and rising', but of a piercing of her soul with a sword. Mary is linked with Israel's experience of falling or rising by the word 'also': 'And a sword will pierce your own soul too'.[49]

The reader recalls an image, from Israel's prophets, of a sword used for the judgment of the Lord passing through the land (see esp. Ezek 14:17). The sword is not one of punishment, but of discrimination, destroying some and sparing others, depending upon their response to the word of God (see also Ezek 5:1-2; 6:8-9; 12:14-16; Is 49:1-2). This is the background for Simeon's parenthetic remark to Mary. Jesus will cause the fall and the rising of many

---

49 The Greek expression *de* which I have translated as 'too' (along with the NRSV) or 'also' (RSV) is disputed by textual critics. The manuscript evidence is finely balanced, and the context leads me to urge its inclusion.

in Israel ... and among the Israelites stands his own mother! She is part of her people: she also will be called to further decisions.[50]

The reader's familiarity with Mary's response from the earlier parts of the narrative guides him or her to read these words of Simeon aware that the use of 'fall' does not apply to the mother of Jesus. She will experience the discriminatory presence of the sword which her son will bring among her people (see Mt 10:34-36).[51] Being an Israelite does not guarantee salvation ... nor does being a member of Jesus' family. Only a never-failing openness to God's ways effects such a guarantee, and Mary has already demonstrated such openness (see especially 1:26-38). At this stage of Luke's narrative, however, Mary's journey of faith is only beginning. It is along this journey of faith that Mary will experience a sword piercing her soul. Without ever fully understanding the mysteries to which she is responding, Mary will be asked to repeat her initial decision: 'Let it be with me according to your word' (1:38).

The world and the language of the old economy return, as Anna is described: worshipping with fasting and prayer night and day (vv. 36-37). But she too recognises that the redemption of Israel is at hand, and gives thanks to God (v. 38).

Although present throughout vv. 22-38, Jesus plays no active role in the story. He is proleptically portrayed as

---

50 See J.A. Fitzmyer, 'Mary in Lucan Salvation History', in *Luke the Theologian*, pp. 57-85.

51 This passage from Matthew was probably drawn from the Q source, common to Matthew and Luke: 'Do not think that I have come to bring peace on earth. I have not come to bring peace *but a sword*'. Luke does not use this passage, but my interpretation of Luke 2:35a would show that he uses 'the sword' with the same meaning in that passage. See R.E. Brown, *Birth*, p. 464.

the one who will cause the fall and the rise of many in
Israel, the turning point of God's history. The old economy, in the persons of Simeon and Anna, recognises that
it may now be dismissed in peace. Mary is again importantly present to the narrative. No matter how complete
her response may have been to God's designs for her, her
fiat does not lift her out of the necessary puzzlement and
pain which arise from such a response. The reader is now
deeply involved in the meeting of heaven and earth, the
gracious but demanding presence of God among us.

7. Reading Luke 2:41-52

After an interlude, during which the narrator covers several
years of Jesus' life in Nazareth (vv. 39-40), the reader begins
the final episode of Luke 1-2 armed with the knowledge
that 'the favour of God' was upon the boy (v. 40). God
is still the key to the right reading of the narrative.

But here Jesus plays an active role. Jesus' presence in
the Temple is the result of a complex process whereby
the young boy is left in Jerusalem while his parents and
their company return to Nazareth (vv. 41-44). The parents
return in search of Jesus, only to find him 'in the Temple, sitting among the teachers, listening to them and
asking them questions' (v. 46), creating amazement through
his understanding and answers (v. 47). Wonder, but necessarily faith, again meet the presence of God through his
agents, this time through the agency of his Son.

Jesus speaks only once in the infancy narrative. Until
this final episode it is not Jesus who is the protagonist
of the first two chapters, but God, the parents of John
the Baptist and Mary. Jesus responds to the understandable concern of his parents: 'How is it that you sought

me? Did you not know that I must be about the affairs of my Father *(en tois tou patros mou dei einai me)* (v. 49).[52] The reader becomes aware that, in Jesus' words, the main figure behind the narrative so far, 'God', is now addressed as 'Father'. Thus the promises made to Mary in 1:35 are being fulfilled: 'The child to be born will be holy; he will be called Son of God'.

The narrative tells of a mother and a father who search for a son, and a son who responds that his life must be determined by the program set for him by his Father who is God. The reader faces a possible clash of worlds: the inbreak of God through the presence of his Son renders vain the anxious questioning of the physical mother of Jesus. The mother and father are unable to understand the words of her son, but the mother repeats her acceptance of their mystery in the same way as she accepted the mystery of his birth: she treasures them in her heart (vv. 50-51). The clash of worlds has been resolved by a radical acceptance of the mystery of God's ways.

Jesus, son of Mary and Son of God now stands at the centre of the story. The reader has had a long preparation for this moment. The story of many encounters between God and human beings has become christological.

---

52 My translation. The Greek is open to several translations. I have chosen the one which I think best fits the author's point of view. For a survey of the possiblities, see R.E. Brown, *Birth*, pp. 475-477. Most modern commentators and translations render 'in my Father's house'. See, for example, R.E. Brown, *Birth*, p. 471; J.A. Fitzmyer, *Luke I-IX*, p. 434; I.H. Marshall, *Luke*, p. 129; RSV; NRSV; TOB; NJB. For my choice, see E. Schweizer, *Luke*, p. 64; G. Schneider, *Lukas*, pp. 75-76; JB. See also C.F. Evans, *Saint Luke*, p. 226, where he discusses this possibility. For an exhaustive survey, see R. Laurentin, *Jésus au Temple. Mystére de Paques et Foi de Marie* (EB; Paris: Gabalda, 1966) pp. 38-72.

The son of Mary is the Son of God. He incarnates the meeting between heaven and earth.[53]

Throughout the narrative Mary has unfailingly responded to the design of God. She treasured these things in her heart, accepting the discriminating sword which will continue to call her to decision. Such is not the case with her son. As the Son of the Father he is the presence of God in history. The tentative attempts of the many characters who appear throughout Luke 1-2 to respond to the challenge of God's entry into the human story, including Mary, have all been surpassed. Jesus is the perfect response to God, as he is the Son of God. There is no stumbling from silence (see 1:29) to reason (see 1:34) to faith (see 1:38). In his first appearance Jesus calls God 'my Father' and he is dominated by a concern for all that pertains to his Father. Through Jesus' response the reader knows that Jesus is now ready to begin his life and ministry. Heaven and earth have met; they have become one in the person of Jesus, son of Mary, Son of God. Jesus of Nazareth embodies the visitation of God.[54]

CONCLUSION

God's ways have been made known to human beings through a series of agents and events. God has been the

---

53 Against an interpretation which suggests that Jesus' being in his Father's house already indicates, in the prologue to the Gospel, Jesus' eventual return to his Father through the ascension. See, for example, E. Laverdiere, *Luke*, pp. 37-39.

54 J.B. Tyson, 'The Birth Narratives and the Beginning of Luke's Gospel', *Sem* 52 (1990) 105, 114-116, misses this point by seeing a link between Luke 1:5-2:52 and the discontinuity found in some Greek plays where 'the speaker in the prologue is a god, who withdraws when humans come on the scene' (p. 105). Many commentators see the 1:41-52 as a transition into the public

prime mover and protagonist throughout the infancy narrative, even though God has never appeared or spoken. His various messengers, particularly Gabriel, Simeon and Anna, have been seen and heard. A transcendent God has effaced himself in favour of his chosen mediators until the final scene, where the Son of God announces his project: he must be about the affairs of his Father. The reader has been prepared for this, as Zechariah has twice announced God's visitation. At the opening of the Benedictus he says: 'Blessed be the Lord God of Israel, for he has visited *(epeskepsato)* and redeeemed his people' (1:68). A little later he promises: 'By the tender mercy of our God the dawn from on high will visit *(episkepsetai)* us from on high, to give light to those who sit in darkness' (vv. 78-79).

The reader now approaches the rest of the narrative of the Gospel aware that the divine visitation is embodied in Jesus. But the reader is also aware of the way in which human beings should respond to it. The reader has been well prepared for a story of promise and fulfilment, of the inevitable victory of the plan of God, despite its rejection, especially from Israel (see 7:30, Acts 2:23; 4:28; 5:38-39; 13:36; 20:27).[55] The reading experience of Luke 1-2 has made the reader aware that God enters the lives of women and men promising salvation, and that humans respond in a variety of ways when heaven and earth meet. The reader is about to read of the perfect human response to heavenly demands in the life of Jesus of Nazareth, the Son who is about the affairs of his Father.

---

ministry. See especially J.A. Fitzmyer, *Luke I-IX*, pp. 434-435. I regard it as the culmination of Luke 1:5-2:52.
55 See R.C. Tannehill, *Narrative Unity*, pp. 20-44.

By the end of the Lukan infancy narrative Jesus has been established as the one who embodies the divine visitation, as Mary embodies the human recognition of it. The reader who emerges from the Lukan infancy narrative will approach the life-story of Jesus as a story of God's visitation, already aware of the nature of the authentic human response.[56]

Towards the close of his public ministry Jesus will lament over Jerusalem: 'You did not know the time of your visitation *(ton kairon tês episkopês sou)*' (19:44). The reader of the infancy narrative has been well prepared for this lament, and cannot remain indifferent to it. The ordered account of the Lukan narrative encourages and confirms commitment to the purposes of God. God's visitation is made known in and through the deeds of Jesus, about whom the reader has already been informed (see Lk 1:1-4).

---

56 See E. Schweizer, *Luke*, p. 17. On the links between the infancy narrative and the rest of the Gospel, see J.B. Tyson, 'The Birth Narratives', pp. 111-114.

5 | BEGINNING THE GOSPEL OF JOHN
JOHN 1:1-18[1]

Mark, Matthew and Luke begin with narratives which have a time line and a plot marked by characters and settings. But the first page of the Fourth Gospel appears to have little of that. The prologue to the Fourth Gospel may have been the last part of the Gospel to receive its definitive shape,[2] yet the positioning of the Johannine prologue at the beginning of the narrative is part of the author's narrative strategy.

The reader comes to the prose narrative section of the Gospel (1:19-20:31) armed with the information provided

---

1   The following study is an abbreviated form of Chapter Two of F.J. Moloney, *Belief in the Word. Reading the Fourth Gospel I: John 1-4* (Minneapolis: Fortress Press, 1992).

2   Research into the pre-history of the Johannine prologue is never-ending. See G. Rochais, 'La Formation du Prologue (Jn 1:1-18)', *ScEs* 37 (1985) 7-9 for a scheme presenting the pre-Johannine hymns of 37 authors from 1922-1983. See pp. 41-44 for the bibliography. See also the study of M. Theobald, *Die Fleischwerdung des Logos. Studien zum Verhältnis des Johannesprologs zum Corpus des Evangeliums und zu 1 Joh* (NTAbh. Neue Folge 20; Münster: Aschendorff, 1988) pp. 54-161.

by the poetic narrative of the prologue, but such information creates questions for the reader. Rudolf Bultmann has sensed this: 'He (the reader) cannot yet fully understand them (motifs in the prologue), but because they are half comprehensible, half mysterious, they arouse the tension, and awaken the *question* which is essential if he is going to understand what is going to be said'.[3]

THE SHAPE OF THE PROLOGUE

Robert Lowth's *de sacra poesi Hebraeorum* (1753) taught subsequent readers of biblical poetry to appreciate the use of parallelism.[4] Firmly situated in a Jewish tradition, it is to be expected that the longest poetic passage in the Gospels should reflect the well-established pattern of parallelism. The author of the Fourth Gospel shapes the reader by means of a wave-like unfolding of his message. A wave runs up onto the beach, only to fall back to gather more strength and more water so that its next rolling motion will carry it further. The author makes a point, coming back to it in the next section, only to develop it further.[5]

John 1:1-18 has three major sections:

I The Word in God becomes the light of the world (vv. 1-5).

3   R. Bultmann, *The Gospel of John* (Oxford: Blackwell, 1971) p. 13. (Parentheses mine, stress Bultmann's).
4   C.K. Barrett, *The Gospel according to St John* (London: SPCK, 1978[2]) pp. 150-151. On parallelism in biblical poetry, see R. Alter, *The Art of Biblical Poetry* (New York: Basic Books, 1985) pp. 3-26.
5   I am influenced in what follows by I. de la Potterie, 'Structure du Prologue de Saint Jean', *NTS* 30 (1984) 354-381. See, for the wave image, M.F. Lacan, 'Le Prologue de saint Jean. Ses thèmes, sa structure, son mouvement', *LumVie* 33 (1957) 97.

II The Word in history (vv. 6-14).

III Jesus Christ present to the faith of the Christian community (vv. 15-18).

Within these three sections, the author states and re-states four themes:

1. The Word is announced and described — the basis of the mystery is stated. This is found in the narrator's proclamation of vv. 1-2 (I), in the narrator's description of the Baptist's witness in vv. 6-8 (II) and in the words of the Baptist in v. 15 (III).

2. The revelation brought by the Word is coming into the world — the Word is the light of the World. This message is found in the first two sections in the words of the narrator in vv. 3-4 (I) and in v. 9 (II).[6] Once the Incarnation is announced so definitively in v. 14, there is no place for further teaching on the coming of the light into the world in section III.

3. Humankind responds to the gift. V. 5b affirms that the darkness has not overcome the light (I), while vv. 10-13 show that one can accept or refuse to accept the Word who comes into the world (II).[7] In v. 16 the fulness of the gift received is described (III).

6   This view comes from my belief that the Word enters the human scene as early as v. 4. See C.K. Barrett, *St John*, p. 149: 'In the analysis the most important question is: At what point does John first refer to the entry of the Word upon the human scene?'

7   I disagree with de la Potterie on v. 13. Following an early patristic tradition, he reads the singular *egennêthê*, and takes it as a reference to the virginal conception. See *ibid.*, pp. 370-372. See F.J. Moloney, *Mary Woman and Mother*, pp. 31-32, note 1, and especially J.W. Pryor, 'Of the Virgin Birth or the Birth of Christians? The Text of John 1:13 once more', *NovT* 27 (1985) 296-318.

4. The object of faith is described – the only Son of the Father. It is too early for such a description in vv. 1-5 (I). Vv. 6-14 conclude with the proclamation of the Word's becoming flesh, the only Son of the Father among us (II). The prologue comes to a close in vv. 17-18 with a further description of the Word. His name is Jesus Christ, and he replaces the former gift of the Law. No one has ever seen God, but the only Son, gazing towards his Father at all times, tells God's story (III).

The author has constructed three parallel passages, deepening and expanding the same essential message with each statement and re-statement.

a) In vv. 1-5 (I) the reader learns of the Word (1), his being the light of humankind (2) and the ultimate helplessness of opposition to that light (3).

b) In vv. 6-14 (II) the Baptist is reported as giving negative witness to the light (1), only the Word is the light of humankind (2), but some accept and some refuse the light (3). The Word, the only Son of God, has become flesh and dwelt among us (4).

c) In vv. 15-18 (III) the Baptist actively proclaims his witness to the Word (1), the all-surpassing nature of the gift we have received is described (3). Jesus Christ, the only Son of God makes God known (4).

The prologue is a thrice-told story of the Word, his coming as the light of humankind, and the response to the gift who is Jesus Christ, the Son of God. This preliminary discussion of the shape of the narrative enables us to present a structured reading of the text itself as follows:

John 1:1-18

I – THE WORD

[1] In the beginning was the Word, and the Word was turned towards God, and what God was the Word was.

[2] He was in the beginning with God.

(1)
The Word

---

[3] (a) All things came into being through him.

(b) and apart from him nothing came into being.

(c) What appeared **[4]** in him was life, and the life was the light of humankind.

(2)
Coming

---

[5] And the light shines in the darkness, and the darkness did not overcome it.

(3)
Reception

II – THE WORD IN HISTORY

[6] There was a man, sent from God, whose name was John.

[7] He came for testimony, to bear witnesss to the light, that all might believe through him.

[8] He was not the light, but came to bear witness to the light.

(1¹)
The Word

[9] The true light that enlightens every man was coming into the world.

(2¹)
Coming

[10] He was in the world, and the world was made through him, yet the world knew him not.

[11] He came to his own home, and his own people received him not.

[12] But to those who received him, to those who believed in his name, he gave power to become children of God;

(3¹)
Reception

[13] who were born, not of blood, nor of the will of the flesh, nor of the will of man, but of God.

[14] (a) And the Word became flesh

(b) and dwelt among us,

(c) and we have looked upon his glory,

(4¹)
Described

(d) glory as of the only Son of the Father:

(e) the fulness of a gift which is truth.

III – THE WORD AMONG US

[15] John bore witness to him, and proclaimed: 'This was he of whom I said, "He who comes after me ranks before me, for he was before me"'.

(1¹)
The Word

[16] And from his fulness have we all received, a gift in place of a gift.	*(3²)* *Reception*

[17] For the law was given through Moses; the gift which is the truth came through Jesus Christ.	*(4²)* *Described*
[18] No one has ever seen God; the only Son, turned towards the bosom of the Father, he has told his story.	

... and this is the testimony of John ... (v. 19).

READING THE PROLOGUE

1. Reading John 1:1-5:
The Word in God and the Light of the World

The reader is sufficiently familiar with Jewish tradition to be aware of the reference to Gen 1:1: 'In the beginning' *(en archê)*. But *before* that *archê* of Gen 1:1 the Word 'was'. The choice of the imperfect form of the verb 'to be' places the Word outside time, without any controlled 'beginning' of his own. In that timeless situation before there ever was time, the Word existed in a relationship: 'and the Word was turned towards God' *(kai ho logos ên pros ton theon)*.[8]

---

8 W. Kelber, 'The Birth of a Beginning: John 1:1-18', *Sem* 52 (1990) 121-144, offers a fascinating post-modern reading of the prologue. He claims that the prologue deconstructs the affirmation *Logos en archê:* the Word in the beginning. In reading v. 1 as 'the Word in the beginning' as insinuating 'foundational stability' (p. 122) Kelber misreads the text to serve deconstruction. John 1:1 is not about 'the Word in the beginning', but a relationship which has always existed between *ho logos and ho theos.*

There is a mutuality involved in a relationship which is difficult to render in succinct English. One must paraphrase to render: 'and the Word was turned towards God'. But the fact that an intimate mutuality is involved is further indicated by the explanation: 'and what God was the Word was' *(kai theos ên ho logos)*. The two parties of the relationship are so close that what one is, the other also is. Yet God and the Word remain distinct. The author has constructed his sentence carefully to inform his reader that the Word is not to be simply identified with God.[9]

The reader is in a world outside time and outside human experience, but the narrator adds: 'He was in the beginning turned towards God'. Who is this 'he'? A more literal translation would read: 'This man *(houtos)* was in the beginning turned towards God'. The reader simply does not have sufficient information from vv. 1-2 to be able to say who 'this man' might be.

Two elements present in vv. 1-2 already hint that the pre-existent Word will have a human story. The first of these is the choice of the term 'the Word'. Discussion over the background to this term goes on apace.[10] But the choice of the Greek expression *ho logos*, whatever its background, allows the author to hint to his reader that from

9 Many important translations (e.g. JB, NJB, RSV, NRSV, BJ, TOB) render: 'the Word was God'. Such a translation is satisfactory as long as the author's distinction between *the* Word and *the* God are clear. See the note in R.E. Brown, *The Gospel According to John* (AB 29; New York: Doubleday, 1966) p. 5, and his further remarks on pp. 24-25.

10 For a survey of the discussion, see R. Schnackenburg, *The Gospel according to St John* (HTCNT IV/1; London: Burns & Oates, 1968) pp. 481-493; C.K. Barrett, *St John*, pp. 152-155. W. Kelber, 'The Birth', pp. 122-130, has subtly returned to the widely rejected (despite the efforts of H. Koester and J.M. Robinson) History of Religions' approach to this question. See also the critical remarks of R.C. Tannehill, 'Beginning to Study "How Gospels Begin" ', *Sem* 52 (1990) 189.

the intimacy between the Word and God which has been
described, 'the Word' will be spoken. A word communicates. If the Word is, then it exists to say something. As
E.C. Hoskyns claims of the use of *ho logos* in the prologue:

> That Jesus once spoke is more fundamental for its
> understanding than is the history of Greek philosophy
> or the story of the westward progress of Oriental mysti-
> cism; more fundamental even than the first chapter of
> Genesis or the eighth chapter of Proverbs ... What the
> Evangelist meant by the Word, what indeed he meant
> by the architecture of his prologue, he has made himself
> known in the body of his work.[11]

The second hint, still puzzling the reader is the *houtos*
of v. 2. Just who might 'this man' be? Does it simply refer
back to *ho logos* in v. 1 or does it look forward into a human
story? The emerging reader reads on to discover who 'this
man' might be. A Word which must be uttered and 'this
man' who may have a history shape a reader who suspects that the pre-existent intimacy described in vv. 1-2
may not be all there is to tell.[12]

Throughout vv. 1-2 the imperfect tense of the verb 'to
be' *(ēn)* is the only verb used, expressing the timeless
ness of the relationship between the Word and God. In
v. 3ab the reader encounters a double use of the aorist
tense *(egeneto)*. The Greek aorist indicates an action, now

---

11 E.C. Hoskyns – F.N. Davey (ed.), *The Fourth Gospel* (London: Faber &
    Faber, 1947) p. 137. See also R. Bultmann, *John*, p. 35: 'From the outset
    God must be understood as 'the one who speaks', the God who reveals
    himself'. This is contrary to Kelber's claim that 'the Word' insinuates foun-
    dational stability.
12 Commenting on v. 1, C.K. Barrett, *St John*, p. 156 correctly notes: 'John
    intends that the whole of his gospel shall be read in the light of this verse.
    The deeds and words of Jesus are the deeds and words of God; if this be
    not true the book is blasphemous'.

concluded, which took place in the past. The affirmation 'All things came into being *(egeneto)* through him, and apart from him nothing came into being *(egeneto)*' (v. 3ab), looks back to the creative act of God in the past.[13] The Word entered the human story at creation. Thus, in creation itself the Word can be seen and experienced (see Wis 13:1; Rom 1:19-20). In vv. 3c-4 the perfect tense replaces the aorists of v. 3ab. The Greek perfect tense also indicates an action from the past, but it is used to indicate that the significance of that action reaches into the present. God's action did not cease in the event of creation (v. 3ab). 'What appeared *(gegonen)* in him was life, and the life was the light of humankind'.[14] Life and light live on in the human story as a result of the Word's appearance there.

The author is giving the reader a brief but dense lesson on the history of salvation which can be plotted from pre-existence of the Word to the life and light brought into history through an identifiable human figure.

1. A pre-existent Word with God (v. 1: *pros ton theon*).

2. God's manifestation *ad extra* (v. 3ab: *di'autou*) wherein the Word can already be experienced.

3. The Word in the human story as the life which is the light of humankind (vv. 3c-4: *en autôi*).

13 See F. Kermode, 'John', in *The Literary Guide*, p. 445: 'The poem is what might be called a 'threshold' poem. It is concerned with what *was* (in Chrysostom's sense, eternally) and how that which *was* crossed over into *becoming*. So the key words of the poem, its axis, are *was* and *became*, the Greek *ên and egeneto*, common words used in an uncommon way'.

14 For an up-to-date and detailed study of the complicated text-critical problems behind vv. 3-4, see Ed. L. Miller, *Salvation-History in the Prologue of John. The Significance of John 1:3-4* (NovTSupp LX; Leiden: E.J. Brill, 1989) pp. 17-44. I am largely following him here.

The Word is in the world as life and light. The Word is the life which is the light of the world. There has been a time of darkness which has now been enlightened by the historical event of a coming of the Word bringing life and light to humankind.[15]

The author can now proceed to the third and final aspect which he wishes to treat in this first part of his story: the response of humankind to the gift it has been given. He does it with a further change in the tense of the main verb used: 'and the light shines (present tense: *phainei*) in the darkness, and the darkness has not overcome (aorist tense: *ou katelaben*) it'. There was an event in the past which may have looked, to the uninformed, like a victory for the powers of evil over the light, but such was not the case (aorist: *ou katelaben*); the light still shines (present: *phainei*).[16]

All of this remains mysterious for the reader. Barnabas Lindars has remarked: 'To the Christian reader the verse already contains a hint of the Passion and Resurrection of Jesus'.[17] Such knowledge is, of course unavailable to a reader to whom the Johannine story is only now being

---

15 See H. van den Bussche, *Jean. Commentaire de l'Evangile Spirituel* (Bruges: Desclée de Brouwer, 1976) p. 83. Very few commentators would accept that the coming of the Word into the human story at v. 4 makes reference to the incarnation of the Word. See especially W. Kelber, 'The Birth', pp. 130-136, whose deconstruction of the *logos* depends upon v. 14 as the beginning of his incarnational mission. It is the third beginning of the prologue, after v. 1 (the Logos) and vv. 6-8 (the Baptist). No consideration is given to the *gegonen* of v. 4 or the *en tôi kosmôi ên* of v. 10. My major problem with this interesting study is the lack of a *close reading* of the text itself.

16 Along with most interpreters, I understand the narrator's use of the verb *katalambanein* as meaning 'overcome', not its other possible meaning 'to grasp intellectually – to comprehend'.

17 B. Lindars, *The Gospel of John* (NCB; London: Oliphants, 1972) p. 87.

told.[18] The reader encounters a first description of the response to the coming of the Word. The reader will have to experience the rest of the story to understand all the implications of the clash between the light and the darkness.

The reader is now aware of the pre-existence of a Word, turned in loving union towards God with such an intensity that what God was, the Word also was (v. 1). But a Word exists to say something *ad extra*, and the Word is enigmatically referred to as 'this man' *(houtos)* who was in the beginning (v. 2). The questioning begins: who is this man? How is the Word spoken? The narrator tells the reader that the Word has already been spoken in the creative action of God (v. 3ab) and in an even more significant further event: in the appearance of a figure in whom life and light may still be found (v. 3c-4). His light has shone during a human story in which the powers of darkness attempted to quench it. But the light shines still (v. 5).

2. Reading John 1:6-14:
The Incarnation of the Word: Son of the Father

The narrator was the first to announce and describe the word, in vv. 1-2. Here the narrator again announces the Word through a description of the figure whom the reader will soon discover is the authentic witness: John the Baptist (vv. 6-8).

The reader is drawn into events of past history with the first words of v. 6: 'a man appeared' (aorist tense: *egeneto*

---

18 The Johannine implied reader can probably be credited with a basic knowledge of the story of Jesus, but is reading the Johannine version of it for the first time. See above, pp. 35-36.

anthrôpos). A man appeared in the past; he is no longer among us. The reader encounters a historical person who had a name − 'his name was John'. Human beings have names, but this is no ordinary human being. He has been 'sent by God' *(apestalmenos para theou)*. In the Fourth Gospel, John the Baptist is the only human figure, apart from Jesus (see 1:14; 6:46; 7:29; 9:16, 33; 16:27; 17:8), associated with God in this way. The reader is introduced to a historical figure who is an 'apostle' of God. This is the author's way of establishing the authenticity of the witness which the Baptist will give to the Word.

Three reasons are given for the Baptist's coming (v. 7) which lead the reader from what has already been learnt into what is yet to come.

1. He came for testimony *(eis marturian)*.

2. He came to bear witness to the light. The reader knows from vv. 3c-4 that only the Word is the light of humankind. The Baptist points to that light, and in doing so gives a further indication to the reader that the light is not the inner workings of a Word-God relationship, but part of the human story.

3. The final reason given for his coming is 'that all might believe through him'. The reader is able to recall that the Word was in God, that it was manifested in creation, and that life and light came only through the Word (vv. 1-4). The reader is now informed that 'belief' (whatever that may mean) must be part of the reception of light and life.

But the narrator states firmly what the Baptist was not: he was not the light. He is the witness to the light, but he is not the light (v. 8).

He can now move to the second theme of the central section of the prologue: the Word is coming into the world (v. 9).[19] Over against the many 'lights', the Word is described as the *true* light. The Word is the uniquely authentic and perfect revelation of God. The present tense of the verb *(phôtizei)* tells the reader that the light is enlightening humankind. As in v. 5 it is, or can be, part of the reader's experience.

The author has first linked the Baptist with the light. He bears witness to the presence of the light in the human story. Now he makes explicit what was implicit in the witnessing of the Baptist: that the light itself was coming into the world. The narrator is making affirmations about the Word, the life, the light and about what the Word brings into the human story. But how, when and where does this take place? The following description of the ways in which the Word is received (vv. 10-13) indicates to the reader that he or she is being introduced to a story about human events which elicit a human response.

In one terse expression, the narrator introduces the reader to a variety of possible meanings for the expression 'the world' *(ho kosmos)*.[20] The reader is told first of

---

19   The Greek *ên to phôs to alêthinon, ho phôtizei panta anthrôpon, erchomenon eis ton kosmon* is open to either: 'He was the true light which enlightens every man coming into the world' or 'The true light, which enlightens every man, was coming into the world'. While the former has good Rabbinic parallels, I am choosing the latter, taking the *ên ... erchomenon* as a periphrastic construction. On this, see ZBG, p. 126. For surveys of the discussion, see R.E. Brown, *John*, pp. 9-10; C.K. Barrett, *St John*, pp. 160-161, and especially J.W. Pryor, 'Jesus and Israel in the Fourth Gospel – John 1:11', *NovT* 32 (1990) 203-204.

20   See, on this, N.H. Cassem, 'A Grammatical and Contextual Inventory of the use of *kosmos* in the Johannine Corpus with some Implications for a Johannine Cosmic Theology', *NTS* 19 (1972-73) 81-91; C.K. Barrett, *St John*, pp. 161-162; R.E. Brown, *John*, pp. 508-510.

the material reality of the created world, which provides the context for the coming of the Word. The Word was in this world (v. 10a).[21] The narrator next refers to a more theological reality of the world which was made through him (v. 10b). It has its origins and gains its sense and purpose through him.[22]

But there is another meaning of *ho kosmos* with which the author climaxes v. 10. Although the reader has already been partially prepared for the theme of the rejection of the Word through the first indication of a conflict between light and darkness in v. 5, the affirmation of v. 10c comes as something of a shock: 'Yet the world knew him not'. The reference to the negative response to the Word in v. 5 is now being further developed. There is a power of evil at large which will not accept the revelation brought by the Word. This power of evil is also called *ho kosmos*.[23]

Repeating the use of the verb 'to come', already found in v. 9, the reader learns that he came 'to his own home'. The imperfect 'was coming' of v. 9, is now an aorist 'he came' in v. 11a. The narrator tells the reader of an event in the past: the historical event of the coming of the Word into history. When that took place, and how it took place, is still a mystery to the reader. However, the narrator makes it clear *that* it took place. The expression 'homeland, true

---

21 The reader will later meet this meaning in 11:9; 17:5, 24; 21:25.
22 The reader will later find that there is a world loved by God (3:16) of which Jesus Christ is saviour (4:42). Jesus takes away the sins of the world (1:29) and his flesh can be the life of the world (6:51). Indeed, he is the light of the world (8:12; 9:5).
23 For the first time the reader meets a sense of 'the world' which will return in 7:7; 14:17, 22, 27, 30; 15:18-19; 16:8, 20, 33; 17:6, 9, 14-16. The life story of Jesus Christ will teach that there is a prince of evil at large in this world (12:31; 14:30; 16:11), whom Jesus Christ overcomes (16:33).

dwelling place' *(ta idia)* was a favourite expression among
the Gnostics to speak of the heavenly spheres into which
the redeemed would eventually return.[24] That was the
real home of the soul, at present lost in the chaos of creation. True to Christian tradition, the author reverses this.
'His own home' is not the heavenly spheres, but the
human story.

His own people *(hoi idioi)* received him not.[25] The
author tells of the negative response of those from the
human story who did not accept the revelation brought
by the Word by using a negative form of the verb 'to
receive' *(paralambanein)*. This is the narrator's second use
of an action word related to the verb 'to receive' *(lambanein)* to speak of response to the Word. In v. 5 the reader
was told that the darkness did not overcome the light
(katalambanein). The root verb has the primary sense of
taking to oneself in a more intimate way.[26] There is more
involved in the response to the Word than intellectual
assent. What it entails is not yet clear to the reader. Thus
far the historical appearance of the Word has only met
with refusal (vv. 5 and 11).

But there is the possibility of a positive response, and
this is indicated for the reader in vv. 12-13. Again we find
the verb 'to receive' *(lambanein)*. In v. 12 it is used in
parallel with the verb 'to believe' *(pisteuein)*:

---

24 On this, see B. Layton, *The Gnostic Scriptures* (London: SCM Press, 1987)
    pp. 12-17, and the references in R. Bultmann, *John*, p. 56, note 1.
25 Related to *ta idia*, in Hellenistic mysticism and Gnosticism *hoi idioi* were
    'the favoured and elect who have received divine revelation and attained
    the goal of union with God'. See R. Schnackenburg, *St John*, pp. 259-260.
    The exact opposite is the case with the use of the term in our text.
26 See BAGD, pp. 464-465.

hosoi de elabon *auton*   *tois* pisteusousin *eis to to onoma autou.*

to those who received him   to those who believed in his name.

The reader was not told in either v. 5 or v. 11 what the correct response to the Word might be, as the response of both the darkness and 'his own people' is reported as an attempt to overcome or refuse the light. On both occasions the reader meets a negation of 'receiving' (v. 5: *ou katelaben*; v. 11: *ou parelabon*). In v. 12 this response is reversed, but further questions emerge. In v. 12 the 'receiving' is clarified: to receive *(elabon)* the Word one must believe *(pisteusousin)* in his name.[27] But in whose name must one believe? The only name which the reader has been given so far is that of John the Baptist (v. 6). The author has made it clear that John is not the light (v. 8) but that he came to bear witness to the Word, 'so that all might believe through him' (v. 7). The further questions now are: what makes for authentic receiving-believing? In whose name must one believe? It must be in the name of the Logos, but as yet the Logos has no name. These questions are related to the 'how' of the revelation of the Word. They will not be resolved within the prologue itself. The reader looks forward to some narrated time when these questions will be resolved in the life-story of a human being.

Receiving the Word, believing in his name, whatever that may mean, and who the Word in history might be, gave power to become children of God. The narrator reports a past event. Some have already been given that power. The verb *(edōken)* is an aorist. The power given is not a promise, a mere possibility, but an achieved fact

---

27 See R. Schnackenburg, *St John*, pp. 261-263.

in the lives of those who received and believed (see 10:18; 17:2). One does not have to wait for the end time to become a child of God; it can be had already if one receives the Word by believing in his name.

In v. 10 *the fact* of the rejection of the world was stated, while in v. 11 the author reported *how* this happened: human arrogance refused to receive the Word. Similarly, v. 12 reports *the fact* that some accept the revelation of the Word. Matching v. 11, but in sharp contrast to it, v. 13 reports *how* this takes place. While in v. 11 the rejection of the Word came from human action and initiative, in v. 13 the reader learns that the believer becomes a child of God through the absolute initiative of God.

In the world which produced and first read the Fourth Gospel there were three possible ways in which one could speak of the production of a newly-born child. First there was the purely physiological belief that a woman fell pregnant from the coagulation of the woman's blood due to the mingling with the male seed.[28] But children of God are not born 'of blood'. Then there was the frailty of the human flesh which must express itself sexually and which consequently produces a child. But children of God are not born 'of the will of the flesh'. Finally, and most nobly, there are those situations where human beings act as human beings and decide on the birth of a child.[29] But children of God are not born 'of the will of a human being'. The children of God are not the result of any human

---

28 As J.H. Bernard, *A Critical and Exegetical Commentary on the Gospel according to St John* (ICC; Edinburgh: T. & T. Clark, 1928) Vol. I, p. 18, has pointed out, the unusual plural *ouk ex haimatôn* is to be understood in the sense of the mixing of the female and the male 'bloods'.

29 E.C. Hoskyns, *Fourth Gospel*, p. 146 refers to this expression as 'a parable of what lies behind human fatherhood'.

initiative. They are born 'of God'. The reader learns that the divine filiation does not result from human initiative, but from the gift of God.

An incarnation of the Word was already behind vv. 3c-5, and presupposed throughout vv. 6-13. As v. 5 closed the first section of the prologue (vv. 1-5) with a reference to the conflict between the powers of light and darkness which takes place in the incarnate word, so also the second section of the prologue (vv. 6-14) concludes with a similar, but even clearer statement for the reader on the incarnation of the Word (v. 14).[30]

The description of the incarnation of the Word in v. 14 is made through five statements. The first of these is the celebrated expression: 'And the Word *became flesh*' (v. 14a). For the first time since vv. 1-2 the expression *ho logos* returns. As the Baptist was introduced into the story through an aorist tense: 'appeared' (see v. 6: *egeneto*), so also the historical appearance of the Word is introduced: 'And the Word became flesh' (v. 14a: *kai ho logos sarx egeneto*). In sharp contrast to the use of the imperfect tense of the verb 'to be' in vv. 1-2, the reader is now told that, like the Baptist, the Word 'appeared', 'happened' on the scene of human events.

There is a variety of uses of the word 'flesh' *(sarx)* in the Fourth Gospel. What the reader will discover, reading further, is that the meaning of the expression depends upon whether it refers to the flesh of Jesus or the flesh of others in the story. The use of the 'flesh' of Jesus is closely related to the Johannine theme of the revelation of God found in the elevation of the body of Jesus on

30 Against W. Kelber, 'The Birth', pp. 130-136.

the Cross (6:51, 52, 53, 54, 55, 56).[31] Such teaching, which depends upon the first reference to the word 'flesh' in v. 14a, is yet to come for the reader. As a virginal reader he or she does not read 'flesh' in either a Pauline or a Gnostic sense. At this stage of the reading process all that can be grasped is that the pre-existent Word (vv. 1-2), in becoming flesh, can be the communication and revelation of God in the human situation, through the enfleshed Logos.[32]

The author's choice of words continues to be significant in his next statement: 'and dwelt among us' *(kai eskênôsen en hêmin)*. The verb used could mean simply 'to dwell' or 'to live', and there is an allusion to the dwelling of Wisdom in Israel: 'The one who created me assigned me a place for my tent. And he said "Make your dwelling *(kataskênôson)* in Jacob, and in Israel receive your inheritance"' (Sir 24:8). It is also possible that the similar sounding Hebrew verb *shâkan* may have helped in the choice of the expression. The verb is used of the dwelling of YHWH in Israel (Ex 25:8; 29:46; Zech 2:14), and a derived word *(shekinah)* is used in Rabbinic Judaism to speak of the resting of the glory (Hebrew: *kabôd*) of YHWH over the Tabernacle (see Ex 24:16; 40:35). If this is the case, it prepares the reader for the later affirmation: 'We have seen his glory' (v. 14d).

The dwelling of the Word, however, is 'among us'. For the first time in the prologue the narrator takes on a role

---

31 On this, see F.J. Moloney, *The Johannine Son of Man*, pp. 87-123 and Idem, 'John 6 and the Celebration of the Eucharist', *DRev* 93 (1975) 243-251.

32 Contrary to R. Bultmann, *John*, pp. 62-66 who argues that taking on base flesh is the lowest point in the humiliation of the Logos: 'The *offence* of the gospel is brought out as strongly as possible' (p. 63). On this discussion, see M.M. Thompson, *The Humanity of Jesus in the Fourth Gospel* (Philadelphia: Fortress Press, 1988) pp. 33-52.

from within a community of believers. The community's experience is reported: 'and we gazed upon his glory' *(kai etheasametha ten doxan autou)*. The choice of the aorist tense of the verb 'to see' *(theasthai)* indicates the experience of a given community of believers who, during the period in which the Word took up his dwelling (complexive aorist), gazed upon the glory. It was not just a look or a glance. R.E. Brown, quoting G.L. Philips approvingly, says of the verb: 'It means to look at some dramatic spectacle and in a measure to become a part of it'.[33] During the historical existence of the Word, believers saw the glory *(doxa)*.

This is the first appearance of another term which will play a large role in the unfolding of the Gospel story. The Old Testament often spoke of the visible manifestation of YHWH to his people in terms of 'glory' (Hebrew: *kabôd*), which was (strangely) rendered in the LXX as the Greek word *doxa* (see, for example, Ex 33:22; Deut 5:21; 1 Kings 8:11; Is 10:1; Hab 2:14). The reader, accredited with a good knowledge of Jewish traditions, understands the Old Testament habit of speaking of the visible presence of God as *kabôd/doxa*. The reader is told that during the earthly appearance of the Word, God manifested himself in a visible way.

A link between v. 14c and vv. 1-2 is made in v. 14d: 'glory as of the only Son from the Father'. In vv. 1-2 a relationship was explained in terms of 'the Word' and 'God'. Now such terms are shifted, in order better to express a relationship which befits a human story: 'Son' and 'Father'. These are the categories Jesus will use throughout the

---

33 R.E. Brown, *John*, p. 502.

Gospel story to speak of the relationship which exists between himself and God. The glory which the Christians gaze upon is the human appearance of the relationship between God and the Word, now expressed as a relationship between Father and Son.

Everything affirmed by the narrator in v. 14abcd could be regarded as a rich summary of a truth which has already been stated in vv. 1-13: the coming of the Word into the world (especially in vv. 4-5 and 9-11). But in v. 14e something new appears. The Word is described in a way which we usually render in English as 'full of grace and truth' *(plêrês charitos kai alêtheias)*. It is almost universally accepted that the expression 'grace and truth' reflects the description of God's loyalty and faithfulness to the covenant and his covenant community in Exodus 34:6 (Hebrew: *hesed we'emeth*). While there may be an allusion to this background, there is more to it.

The Word is described as a fulness. Is there not a danger, however, that we might be understanding the author as if he were Paul in our traditional translation: 'full of grace and truth'? Does 'grace' *(charis)* in the Fourth Gospel mean what it meant for Paul? Behind Paul and John stands a Greek word which means, quite simply, an unsolicited gift.[34] The reader, who is not the product of a Christian culture where the Pauline notion of *charis* as 'grace' would be taken for granted, reads that the Word is the fulness of a gift. What then of the 'and truth' *(kai alêtheias)*? The copulative *kai* need not simply indicate an accumulation of things: gift *and* truth. A second noun, joined to another noun in the same case by *kai* can also be an explanation

34 See LSJ, pp. 1978-1979; BAGD, 877-888.

of the former. The author is telling his reader that the Word is 'the fulness of a gift which is truth'.[35] The emerging reader is being drawn further into the story, as gaps in the narrative increase and questions are posed. To what might this gift and this truth refer? The reader will not have long to wait for the beginnings of an answer, as the question is resumed in vv. 16-17.

The reader comes to the end of the second section of the prologue to the Fourth Gospel firmly situated within the realms of human history. John the Baptist, an identifiable human being with a name, is the God-sent witness to the Word as the only true light (vv. 6-8). Although the reader has already been told that the Word is the light of humankind (v. 4), he or she is now further informed that the light is actually coming upon the stage of human drama: the world (v. 9). Vv. 1-5 were dominated by the pre-existent relationship which has existed from before human time between the Word and God. This Word is now a part of the human story which is, nevertheless, always free; always able to accept or reject the Word. Although the reader knows no more of the story than what has been read so far, the reader is informed that the Word's presence among his own people in his own homeland met rejection (vv. 10-11). How can this be? The reader must wait for the narrated time of the future to resolve that question.

But some do accept the Word. They make him their own by believing in him. They are given an exquisite gift from God: they become his children (vv. 12-13). How

---

35 For a detailed study of this question, see I. de la Potterie, '*Charis* paulinienne et *charis* johannique' in E.E. Ellis – E. Grässer (eds.), *Jesus und Paulus. Festschrift für Werner Georg Kümmel zum 70. Geburtstag* (Göttingen: Vandenhoeck und Ruprecht, 1975) pp. 256-282.

this happens for the characters in the story and for the reader will also be revealed in future narrated time. The narrator, however, insists from experience that the Word became part of the human story. In doing so he perfected all the gifts of God, enabling the narrator and fellow believers to look upon the revelation of God himself in the incarnate Word, the Son of the Father (v. 14). The narrator is making massive affirmations which the reader must accept, but they leave him wondering: how can this be?

3. Reading John 1:15-18: The Revealer: the only Son turned towards the Father

John the Baptist bears witness in direct speech. The message of vv. 6-8 is recalled as he insists upon the secondary nature of his role, but more important is the positive recalling of the initial description of the Word in vv. 1-2. In terms of the temporal sequence of events which are used to determine the human story, there is one who is coming after John. But he existed before him. The Baptist himself speaks from his place in time and history to the reader, telling him how this is possible: 'because he *was* before me' *(hoti prôtos mou ên)*. The repeated use of the imperfect form of the verb 'to be' to describe the Word in vv. 1-2 is recalled.

After all that has been said, and after the synthesis of v. 14a, the coming of the Word is no longer narrated. Looking back to the 'fulness of a gift which is truth' in v. 14e, the narrator reflects the context of a believing Christian community to claim: 'And from his fulness we have all received' (v. 16). The response of the community has been to receive the gift offered.

The 'fulness' of the Word is a gift given to the believer. In the later Gnostic systems 'the fulness' *(to plêrôma)* was a distant and lost reality for which the soul yearned.[36] The expression *charis* retains the meaning I gave it v. 14e: an unsolicited gift. From his fulness, the believing community has received a free and unsolicited gift which has replaced a former free and unsolicited gift. The two gifts are described: 'For the Law was given through Moses' (v. 17a). There can be no lessening the importance of the former gift. It was from God and it was fundamental for the people of God. Moses was its mediator. However, it was the *former* gift. There is now another gift which has taken its place, the gift which is the truth which 'took place' (aorist: *egeneto*) through Jesus Christ.[37] A name has now been given to the Word. He is Jesus Christ.

The emerging reader is being led into a life-story. A human being with a name and a role, Jesus the Christ, has a story. However, the reader begins a reading of the life-story armed with the knowledge that all that has been said of the Word can now be said of Jesus Christ. How can this be? It is one thing to affirm that the Logos is Jesus the Messiah, but how does this man live out his messianic role? So many unresolved questions remain. The reader must press on into the story of the life and death of Jesus.

The conclusion to the prologue (v. 18) both continues the final description of the gift of the Word in Jesus Christ,

---

36 See especially G. Filoramo, *A History of Gnosticism* (Oxford: Blackwell, 1990) pp. 101-141. See also B. Layton, *The Gnostic Scriptures*, pp. 12-17.
37 See W. Kelber, 'The Birth', pp. 138-140.

and introduces the reader to the narrative of the Gospel which follows.[38]

An emphatic pronoun *(ekeinos)* claims that there is only one who has made God known (v. 18c). The only Son has made the invisible known.[39] In the Greek, the author indicates to his reader that the Son is able to make God known because he is *eis ton kolpon tou patros*. Many scholars rightly see a link between the expression and the 'turned towards God' of v. 1 and subsequently translate the above Greek phrase as 'in the bosom of the Father'. But the narrator is not telling the reader of the life of the Son *in* the Father outside time. Jesus Christ, the only begotten Son, during his historical existence, was turned, looking to his Father. As the union of the Word and God was described outside time in v. 1, the same union is further described in v. 18. But we are now at the end of the prologue. Jesus Christ as the only begotten Son of the Father, makes that Father known to the world through the life which he lives in an unfailing openness and obedience to him. Throughout his life in history, Jesus Christ looks constantly to the Father (see especially 4:34; 5:17-30; 10:30; 17:4). Thus v. 18 describes the enduring intimacy of the union between the Father and the historical Jesus Christ.

Jesus Christ is the gift in whom the truth has taken place because he makes God known through his life-story.

---

38 On the role of 1:18 as a bridge into the life-story of Jesus, see G.R. O'Day, *Revelation in the Fourth Gospel. Narrative Mode and Theological Claim* (Philadelphia: Fortress Press, 1986) pp. 33-35.

39 There are good witnesses which read 'the only God' instead of 'the only Son'. For a discussion of this, see R.E. Brown, *John*, p. 17 (Brown reads 'God the only Son'); R. Schnackenburg, *St John*, pp. 280-282 (Schnackenburg reads 'the only Son'). Schnackenburg (p. 279) comments: 'Whether one reads *theos* or *huios* after *(ho) monogenês* makes no essential difference'. Similarly, C.K. Barrett, *St John*, p. 169.

The invisible God can now be seen in the story of Jesus Christ. In his conclusion to the prologue and transition into the narrative of the life-story of Jesus (v. 18) the narrator tells the reader that:

a) No one in the human story has ever seen God (see also 5:37; 6:46; 1 Jn 4:12-20).

b) The only Son is turned towards the Father in love and obedience throughout the whole of his *historical* presence among women and men (see especially 4:34 and 17:4).

c) He has told God's story in the *historical* events of his life and death.

The reader next encounters the word 'and' (v. 19: *kai*). The reader is led by the author into a reading of the narrative which will tell of those historical events. The narrative must make sense of the prologue, as the prologue has been written to make sense of the narrative.[40]

In vv. 15-18 the poetic narrative speaks directly to the situation of the reader. John the Baptist addresses him in direct speech, re-affirming the pre-existence and the primacy of the Word (v. 15). The narrator, addressing the reader as 'we' (v. 16), speaks of the gift of the fulness of the truth which has taken place in Jesus Christ, a gift from God which has replaced the former gift of the Law. The Word is Jesus Christ, and his closeness to the Father, even during his earthly ministry, enables him to tell the story of the unseen God among us (vv. 17-18).

---

40 Rightly C.K. Barrett, 'The Prologue of St John's Gospel', in *New Testament Essays* (London: SPCK, 1972) p. 48: 'The Prologue is necessary to the Gospel as the Gospel is necessary to the Prologue. The history explicates the theology, and the theology interprets the history'.

The reader has been told that, in the God-planned sequence of events, the Baptist comes 'before' Jesus (see v. 15)
to render testimony (see vv. 6-8). These events did not
happen during the prologue; they were simply affirmed, and
the reader was left wondering *how* they might take place.
Now, connected with 'and', the poetic narrative becomes
prose narrative; the promise of the prologue becomes narrated
event: 'and this is the testimony of John' (v. 19).

CONCLUSION

The reader begins to read a narrative, closely linked to
the prologue through the conjunctive 'and', informed that
the Word exists from all time, turned in loving union
towards God (vv. 1-2), announced and described in history
by the reliable testimony of John the Baptist (vv. 6-8; 15).
The Word comes into the world (vv. 3-4; 9), a gift from
God which can either be accepted or refused (vv. 5; 10-13;
16). This gift is the fulness of God's gracious gifts, sur-
passing even the great gift of the Law through Moses:
the fulness of the gift which is the truth, Jesus Christ
(vv. 14; 17). The life story of Jesus Christ has made God
known (v. 18).

While pre-existence and the Messiah as the glory of
God are exalted claims, they are not foreign to the reader
who is credited with a knowledge of Jewish thought. But
the reader is being further shaped through the information
that the Messiah is *Jesus*. Can this be true? Answers to
this question can only be found through a narrative telling of facts which match the theory: a life-story of Jesus
which shows that he does reveal the glory of God.

The reader is now part of the drama of the narrative
which is about to begin. The reader cannot be indifferent.

He or she now reads on into the life-story of Jesus Christ in the light of the prologue. They may or may not match. That remains to be seen. To be given information – however beautifully and profoundly that communication takes place – is not the end of the questioning. The author has shaped a reader who has been informed that the Word became flesh in the person of Jesus who is the Christ. The reader who emerges at the end of the prologue is aware that the theology of the Word has become the theology of Jesus Christ.

The Word comes on stage with a complete absence of preliminaries. Who is the Word? What is the Word? Where does he hail from? How does he show himself to be divine, as right from the start the author tells us that he and God are one? Can the man Jesus be the Messiah? Such questions are anything but a matter of idle curiosity ... The complex of features making up the Word's portrait emerges only by degrees and only through the action itself.[41]

The reader begins a narrative designed to draw him more deeply into the privileged experience of a community of believers which the implied author claims to represent: 'We have gazed upon his glory ... From his fulness we have all received' (vv. 14 and 16). It is the desire of the real author to shape an implied reader who addresses an intended reader. The author desires that, by entering into the rhetorical contract of the Fourth Gospel, the intended reader, who has not gazed upon the glory (see 20:29), might come to believe that Jesus is the Christ, Son of God, and by believing might have life in his name (see 20:30-31).

---

41 See M. Sternberg, *The Poetics of Biblical Narrative. Ideological Literature and the Drama of Reading* (Indiana Literary Biblical Series; Bloomington: Indiana University Press, 1985) p. 322.

EPILOGUE

The readings of the beginnings of the Four Gospels which I have offered suggest that the Gospels are all marked by what Edward Said has called 'transitive beginnings'. He defines them as 'beginning with (or for) an anticipated end, or at least expected continuity'.[1] But they have also shown that the continuing story and its ending are not contained in the beginning. There is much still to be discovered through the reader's experience of the narrative which follows the beginning. The beginnings of the Gospels are not a 'cryptic summary' of what is to follow.[2] While they provide a great deal of information for the reader, they also raise fundamental questions. They set up a tension in a reader who has learnt from the beginning, but still has more to learn before he or she can rest satisfied.[3]

1 E. Said, *Beginnings. Intention and Method* (New York: Basic Books, 1975) pp. 72-73.
2 See R.C. Tannehill, 'Beginning to Study', p. 187.
3 Not all Gospels will 'end' satisfactorily either. This is especially true of Mark 16:1-8. On 'endings', see J.R.R. Tolkien, *Tree and Leaf*, pp. 60-61. He also comments perceptively on 'the endlessness of the World of Story' (p. 69).

My study of the beginnings of the Four Gospels has led me to conclude that all four can be seen as making a remarkable claim: the God of Israel is God but Jesus Christ is his presence in the human story. Mark does this by having God at the centre of the action throughout the prologue (Mk 1:1-13), but gradually transferring to Jesus titles and activities originally exclusive to YHWH. At the end of the prologue Jesus, the Son in whom the Father is well pleased (1:11), stands actively present in the story, initiating the new creation: with the wild beasts and ministered to by angels (1:13). How will God be pleased with him? How will he bring about the new creation?

Although Jesus appears towards the end of the prologue to the Gospel of Matthew (1:1-4:11. See 3:13-4:11), he does not play an active role in the infancy stories (chs 1-2). Much is said about him, but it points out of the time of the story into future narrated time. God, through the angel of the Lord and the word of the prophets, directs every action in the narrative. Jesus is described as the fulfilment of God's design. The women in the genealogy, Joseph and the wise men from the east show the reader how one should respond to God's promises. How will the story of Jesus show him to be the fulfilment of God's promises, and how will the reader respond to this fulfilment?

Luke's more complex infancy narrative tells a story of the visitation of God: heaven and earth meet. But when heaven meets earth there is a possible clash of worlds. This clash is resolved by the radical and joyful acceptance of its strangeness by Mary, Zechariah, Elizabeth, Simeon and Anna. In the final scene (2:41-52) Jesus incarnates the visitation of God, his Father. He must be about the affairs of his Father (2:49). The reader proceeds into the narrative asking how this visitation will take place and how one should respond. The reader has also been warned of the danger of not knowing the time of God's visitation (2:34-35. See 19:44).

Even the prologue to the Fourth Gospel (Jn 1:1-18), so often seen as the christological high-point of the New Testament, is really about the revelation of God, not Jesus. The reader has no notion about 'who' the Logos might be. The reader is made aware of the dignity of the Logos' unique closeness to God and the function of the Logos as the one who brings life, light and enables those who believe in him to be children of God. The Logos does this by making known the unseen God. But the name 'Jesus Christ' does not appear until the very end of the hymn. The remarkable claim of the prologue is that Jesus Christ is the Word (v. 17) who is so close to God that what God is the Word also is (vv. 1-2).[4] Once again, the reader asks the question: how is this possible? Only the story of the life, teaching, death and resurrection of Jesus which follows will provide an answer.

My study of the beginnings of the four canonical Gospels has not devoted much attention to their 'form',[5] but it appears to me that they can all be seen as serving the same basic 'function': they inform the reader of the 'who' or the 'what' of the story, but they only provide hints concerning the 'how'. This applies both to the subsequent hero of the story, Jesus, and the nature of the reader's response to the events which will be narrated.

---

4   On this, see F.J. Moloney, Art. 'Johannine Theology', *NJBC*, p. 1420.
5   On this, see D.E. Smith, 'Narrative Beginnings', pp. 1-7; J.B. Tyson, 'The Birth Narratives', pp. 103-109.

I am aware that my 'approach' to these beginnings is somewhat classical.[6] It is a mixture of both traditional historical-critical and the more recent literary methods. I sense that such a blend of approaches has much to offer contemporary Gospel studies.

If God is so important, does this modify some of the christological claims which have been made for the Gospel prologues, especially the infancy narratives and John 1:1-18? The careful reader of this book may have noticed from the footnotes that I have already published on Matthew 1-2 and Luke 1-2, but that my Melbourne College of Divinity lectures have led me to abandon the conclusions of my earlier research. I might now add that I was forced to re-write the whole of my lecture on Matthew 1-2 on the morning of the lecture. I had originally written a safe paper, stressing the high Christology of Matthew's infancy narrative, but found that such an approach did not tell the story of its main protagonist: God. This is the great value of the newer approaches now evolving. We have all had the experience of the need to return to important texts, finding that we go on saying the same (tried/tired) things. I now discover that I am able to read these texts with fresh eyes. The promise of the Johannine Jesus comes instantly to mind: 'I have yet many things to say to you, but you cannot bear them now. When the Spirit of truth comes, he will guide you into all truth' (Jn 16:12-13).

I was educated in an older school, where it was generally thought that we could best understand Jesus of Nazareth and the early Church's belief in Jesus Christ

---

6 For a discussion of 'form', 'function' and 'approach', see E.S. Malbon, 'Ending at the Beginning', pp. 175-184.

by means of the rediscovery of authentic material embedded in the narratives, and especially through the titles of Jesus. [7] From the implicit Christology of Jesus' own understanding of himself, one could move to the explicit use of titles (especially 'Son of Man', 'Son' and 'Messiah') in the New Testament, into the early Church and eventually into the the christological confessions of the great Councils. [8] The prologues to all four Gospels provided a wealth of such titles.

I was warned against too rigid an adherence to that approach through the revolution in the study of the parables which marked the 70's. [9] Jesus is not best understood as a figure upon whom titles of honour were eventually heaped; he is the parable of God. [10] I now find that a narrative approach to the beginnings of all four Gospels makes a crucial but different christological claim: the traditional God revealed to and through Israel is the Lord of creation and history, but God has been present

7   See, for example, my 1975 doctoral thesis, *The Johannine Son of Man* (BibScR 14; Rome: LAS, 1978²), especially pp. 208-220. For my further study of the Johannine titles, see F.J. Moloney, *The Word Became Flesh* (Theology Today Series 14; Butler: Clergy Book Service, 1977).

8   The classical examples of this approach are O. Cullmann, *The Christology of the New Testament* (London: SCM Press, 1963²); R.H. Fuller, *The Foundations of New Testament Christology* (London: Lutterworth, 1965); F. Hahn, *Christologische Hoheitstitel. Ihre Geschichte im frühen Christentum* (FRLANT 83; Göttingen: Vandenhoeck & Ruprecht, 1966³).

9   Particularly influential for me were two books by J.D. Crossan: *The Dark Interval. Towards a Theology of Story* (Niles: Argus Communications, 1975) and *In Parables. The Challenge of the Historical Jesus* (San Francisco: Harper & Row, 1973). See now the excellent study of B.B. Scott, *Hear Then the Parable. A Commentary on the Parables of Jesus* (Minneapolis: Fortress Press, 1989). See also C.L. Blomberg, 'Interpreting the Parables of Jesus: Where Are We and Where Do We Go from Here?', *CBQ* 53 (1991) 50-78.

10 See, for example, J.R. Donahue, 'Jesus as the Parable of God in the Gospel of Mark', *Int* 32 (1978) 369-386.

in our larger story in the person of Jesus of Nazareth. To understand *how* this took place, and to understand further *how* one should respond to such good news, one must read his story as each Evangelist's implied author-narrator tells it.

Although written of the beginnings of non-biblical literature, the words of Robert Pope ring true for me, as I come to an end of my study of beginnings of the Good News: 'When I hear the truest voice, I listen, for I feel as though I have been led to the heretofore unknown entrance to underground passageways lighted only by the brilliance of the image opened inside the flow of language. I am afraid to turn back having gone as far as these beginnings, because I have only so many years left to discover the permutations of the internal truth that requires the inward turning of the eyeballs, the truth hidden in the life and voice of another human being, the truth of which we are all seed'.[11]

The beginnings of the Gospels summon us to look inward towards 'the truth of which we are all seed', but they do more. By focusing upon God's initiative and God's presence in the human story through Jesus, Gospel beginnings remind us that we are 'refracted light through whom is splintered from a single White to many hues, and endlessly combined in living shapes that move from mind to mind' (J.R.R. Tolkien).

---

11 R. Pope, 'Beginnings', *The Georgia Review* 36 (1982) 736.

A BRIEF BIBLIOGRAPHY

The following bibliography lists some major works in English. It does not pretend to be exhaustive. I have divided it into two parts. In the first section I list books and articles which deal with narrative criticism as such. Part two indicates some recent works which apply narrative critical theory to New Testament texts.

1. NARRATIVE CRITICAL THEORY

Booth, W.C., *The Rhetoric of Fiction* (Chicago: University of Chicago Press, 1983²).

Chatman, S., *Story and Discourse. Narrative Structure in Fiction and Film* (New York: Ithaca, 1978).

Culler, J., *On Deconstruction. Theory and Criticism after Structuralism* (London: Routledge & Kegan Paul, 1983).

Culler, J., *Structuralist Poetics. Structuralism, Linguistics and the Study of Literature* (London: Routledge & Kegan Paul, 1975).

Fish, S., *Is There a Text in this Class? The Authority of Interpretative Communities* (Cambridge: Harvard University Press, 1988).

Fowler, R.M., 'Who is 'the Reader' in Reader-Response Criticism?', *Semeia* 31 (1985) 5-23.

Freund, E., *The Return of the Reader. Reader-Response Criticism* (New Accents; London: Methuen, 1987).

Genette, G., *Narrative Discourse. An Essay in Method* (Ithaca: Cornell University Press, 1980).

Genette, G., *Narrative Discourse Revisited* (Ithaca: Cornell University Press, 1988).

Iser, W., *The Act of Reading. A Theory of Aesthetic Response* (London: Routledge & Kegan Paul, 1978).

Rimmon-Kenan, S., *Narrative Fiction: Contemporary Poetics* (New Accents; Methuen: London, 1983).

Steiner, G., *Real Presences. Is there anything in what we say?* (London: Faber & Faber, 1989).

Uspensky, B., *The Poetics of Composition: The Structure of the Artistic Text and Typology of a Compositional Form* (Berkeley: University of California Press, 1973).

2. NARRATIVE CRITICISM AND THE BIBLE

Alter, R. - Kermode, F. (eds.), *The Literary Guide to the Bible* (London: Collins, 1987).

Alter, R., *The Art of Biblical Narrative* (New York: Basic Books, 1981).

Bar-Efrat, S., *Narrative Art and the Bible* (JSOTSS 70. Bible and Literature Series 17; Sheffield: Almond Press, 1989).

Berlin, A., *Poetics and Interpretation of Biblical Narrative* (Sheffield: Almond Press, 1989).

Culpepper, R.A., *Anatomy of the Fourth Gospel. A Study in Literary Design* (Foundation and Facets; Philadelphia: Fortress Press, 1983).

Culpepper, R.A., 'Commentary on Biblical Narratives', *Forum* 5,3 (1989) 87-102.

Edwards, R.A., *Matthew's Story of Jesus* (Philadelphia: Fortress Press, 1985).

Frye, N., *The Great Code: The Bible and Literature* (New York: Harcourt and Brace, 1982).

Gerhardt, M., 'The Restoration of Biblical Narrative', *Sem* 46 (1989) 13-29.

Howell, D.B., *Matthew's Inclusive Story. A Study in the Narrative Rhetoric of the First Gospel* (JSNTSS 42; Sheffield: JSOT Press, 1990).

Josipovici, G., *The Book of God. A Response to the Bible* (New Haven: Yale University Press, 1988).

Keegan, T.J., *Interpreting the Bible. A Popular Introduction to Biblical Hermeneutics* (New York: Paulist Press, 1985) pp. 92-109.

Kelber, W., *Mark's Story of Jesus* (Philadelphia: Fortress Press, 1979).

Kelber, W., 'Narrative as Interpretation and Interpretation of Narrative: Hermeneutical Reflections on the Gospels', *Sem* 39 (1987) 107-133.

Kingsbury, J.D., *Matthew as Story* (Philadelphia: Fortress Press, 1988²).

Kinsbury, J.D. *Conflict in Luke. Jesus, Authorities, Disciples* (Minneapolis: Fortress Press, 1991).

Kingsbury, J.D., *Conflict in Mark. Jesus, Authorities, Disciples* (Minneapolis: Fortress Press, 1989).

Marshall, C.D., *Faith as a theme in Mark's narrative* (SNTSMS 64; Cambridge: University Press, 1989).

McKnight, E.V., (ed.), *Reader Perspectives on the New Testament* (Semeia 48; Atlanta: Scholars Press, 1989).

McKnight, E.V., *Post-Modern Use of the Bible. The Emergence of Reader-Oriented Criticism* (Nashville: Abingdon, 1988).

McKnight, E.V., *The Bible and the Reader: An Introduction to Literary Criticism* (Philadelphia: Fortress Press, 1985).

Moloney, F.J., *Belief in the Word. Reading the Fourth Gospel I: John 1-4* (Minneapolis: Fortress Press, 1992).

Moloney, F.J., 'Narrative Criticism of the Gospels', *Pac* 4 (1991) 180-201.

Moore, S.D., *Literary Criticism and the Gospels. The Theoretical Challenge* (New Haven: Yale, 1989).

Morgan, R. - Barton, J., *Biblical Interpretation* (OBS; Oxford: University Press, 1988) pp. 133-296.

Myers, C., *Binding the Strong Man. A Political Reading of Mark's Story of Jesus* (Maryknoll: Orbis, 1990).

Petersen, N.R., *Literary Criticism for New Testament Critics* (GBSNT; Philadelphia: Fortress Press, 1978).

Phillips, G.A. (ed.), *Poststructural Criticism and the Bible: Text/History/Discourse* (Semeia 51; Atlanta: Scholars Press, 1990).

Powell, M.A., *What Is Narrative Criticism?* (GBSNT; New Testament Series; Minneapolis: Fortress Press, 1990).

Smith, D.E. (ed.), *How Gospels Begin* (Semeia 52; Atlanta: Scholars Press, 1990).

Prickett, S., *The Words and the Word. Language, Poetics and Biblical Interpretation* (Cambridge: University Press, 1986).

Rhoads, D. - Michie, D., *Mark as Story. An Introduction to the Narrative of a Gospel* (Philadelphia: Fortress Press, 1982).

Sternberg, M., *The Poetics of Biblical Narrative: Ideological Literature and the Drama of Reading* (Indiana Literary Biblical Series; Bloomington: Indiana University Press, 1985).

Tannehill, R.C., *The Narrative Unity of Luke-Acts. A Literary Interpretation* (2 vols.; Foundation and Facets; Phildelphia/Minneapolis: Fortress Press, 1986-1990).

van Iersel, B. *Reading Mark* (Edinburgh: T. & T. Clark, 1989).

Waetjen, H.C., *A Reordering of Power. A Socio-Political Reading of Mark's Gospel* (Minneapolis: Fortress Press, 1989).

Wilder, A.N., *The Bible and the Literary Critic* (Minneapolis: Fortress Press, 1991).

INDEX OF AUTHORS